The Portage Trail
and Other Journeys

John C. Dailey

Collected Verse 1963 – 2024

Also By John C. Dailey

AUTOBIOGRAPHICAL

The Charles L. Sommers Wilderness Canoe Base:
A Reminiscence

Canoeing Around Hunter's Island via Beaverhouse

October Surprise:
Canoeing with the Wind, Ice and Snow in the BWCA

My First Canoe Trip

Reflections on Canoeing in the Quetico

Pat and John's Fiftieth Wedding Anniversary Book

A Canoe Country Memoir
Sixty Years of Canoeing in the Quetico-Superior 1956–2015

PRESENTATION

The American Chesterton Society Annual Meeting,
Mundeline, Illinois, August 1, 2014. *"Chesterton at Notre Dame,*
October-November, 1930"

FICTION

Bennie the Woodchuck and the Gold Cup

The Story of Gunnar Hansen

POETRY

The Portage Trail and Other Journeys vols. 1, 2, and 3

This book is dedicated to Patricia Ann Dailey,
my loving wife, my best friend, and my muse
for more than sixty years.

Acknowledgements

Once again I have been privileged to work with Dr. James Veenstra, my friend and former colleague, who retired from medicine to pursue, full-time, his career as a fine art photographer and printer. Jim has been able to navigate the intricacies of digital publishing and this book is a byproduct of his expertise. Much kudos is also due to my son, Sean, my daughter, Ellen, and my dear friend, Mara Persic, for their painstaking review of the book and their many helpful suggestions. I also wish to thank my designer, Caroline Kiser, for transforming the book into a beautiful finished product. Finally, I am also indebted to my wife, Patricia, for her encouragement and support.

January, 2017
October 2019, 2nd edition,
and July 2022, 3rd edition

Contents

John C. Dailey

Preface

Over the past few years I have been gathering together some of the poems that I began writing in 1963, my first year in medical school. Most of my early poems were filed away and in fact I had forgotten about them.

About thirty years ago, I started writing more often, motivated by a number of things that were happening in my life, including my four children growing up, the birth of my first grandson, and my involvement with the St. John Fisher Forum, a Catholic speakers' forum that my wife and I founded in 1995. These and other events provided rich fodder for subject material. About that time, it seemed like a door that had been closed gradually opened, and I could see images heretofore unseen. This has been especially true in the past ten years with the world in such a topsy-turvy state.

What you will find in this collection of verse is a brief look at some of the people, places, and things that I have encountered in my life. Hopefully these stories will provide future generations a better understanding of the author. One thing you may discover in reading the poems is that I am a conservative, a traditional Roman Catholic, and am proud of my Irish heritage.

In my youth I was privileged to have spent a number of summers guiding canoe trips in the Boundary Waters Canoe Area in northern Minnesota, and the Quetico Provincial Park in Canada. It was an exciting time, living the life of the historic French Canadian Voyageurs. That experience, along with my Catholic Faith, has shaped my life to the present time.

One of the important aspects of a canoe trip involves moving from lake to lake carrying your canoe and gear over portages, trails through the woods that connect the various lakes. Some portages are short and easy, and some are long and arduous, and you have to be vigilant to stay on the path so as not to get lost. Just as portages are a fact of life in the canoe country, as I have aged and achieved a more mature perspective on the world, I have come to realize that our journey through life is like one long portage. To survive and make it safely to the end, we have to stay on the trail, not an easy thing to do. Anyway that's my philosophy, for what it's worth, and thus the reason for the title of this book.

John C. Dailey

One final thought: the book is divided into four sections because as
I started to collect the material, the subjects discussed seemed to
separate themselves that way. I will provide a brief introduction to each
of the sections and explain more about the poems in that section. The
photographs, art work, and illustrations are included to highlight some of
the poems, hopefully making the book more interesting. Credits are listed
at the end of the book.

—John C. Dailey, January 2017

This second edition of "Portage Trails and Other Journeys" introduces 18
new poems which have been written over the past two years. Ten new
pictures have been added to compliment some of the poems. The theme of
the book remains the same, namely stay on the portage trail if you want to
reach your final destination safely. I am again indebted to Dr. James Veenstra
for his excellent photographic reproductions and to Caroline Kiser Green,
whose design work has resulted in a beautiful finished product, and to my
wife, Pat, for her helpful and timely suggestions and her patience.

—John C. Dailey, October 2019

In this third edition of the "Portage Trails and Other Journeys," I have added
six new poems and a picture of Sea Oats at Pawleys Island that I took. One
of the purposes of these new poems is to introduce the latest additions to
our family, three beautiful great granddaughters who have all been born in
the past year. I have also added three more birthday poems for my grand
daughter, Jane. I would be remiss if I did not acknowledge the continued
support from Jim Veenstra, Caroline Green and my wife, Pat.

—John C. Dailey, Summer 2022

For the fourth edition of "The Portage Trail and Other Journey's," ten new
poems have been added along with new John Payton paintings for the front
and back covers. This edition is being published by Amazon in both a soft
cover and Kindle format. Once again thanks are due to Jim Veenstra and
Caroline K. Green, along with Polly Letofsky, who have been instrumental
in the successful completion of the project. Thanks also to my wife, Pat, for
reviewing the new poems.

John C. Dailey, Summer, 2024

Part One
Marriage and Family

JCDAILEY '82

Part One Contents

John C. Dailey

"

Introduction: Marriage and Family

This group of poems is placed at the beginning of the book for the simple reason that this is where my life as a poet began: when I started medical school and met my future wife. She was the inspiration for the first poem that I wrote, "Happiness," on the occasion of her twenty-second birthday. The rest of the poems recall our dating days, our marriage and some of her birthdays, and the birthdays of some of our children and grandchildren. The "Lost Child" shows how we felt when one of our sons abandoned our family. The two poems, "The Christmas Visitors" and "Christmas Eve" recall a time when I was growing up.

John C. Dailey

My Dream

One day I looked and saw you standing there.
I touched your soft warm skin and couldn't help but stare
Into your sparkling eyes so blue and fair,
Your ruby lips so firm and fine.
We kissed, and for a while time
Stopped. Then you were gone as my alarm began to chime.

John C. Dailey

First Dance

As l reflect on days gone by
And think of you, dear Pat, l
Wonder where the time has gone. ls it just me?
Have l somehow lost my way upon this sea
Of married life that we began so long ago?

Why it was only yesterday when we
First met and danced the Twist. l can still see
That brown-haired lass of twenty-two
Standing there before me thinking, "Who
ls that blond-haired lad of twenty-three?"

The First Day of Spring

I saw a robin sitting on a limb
With bitter gray skies and sunlight dim.
"It's cold outside," I said to him.

Then he glided to the ground
And hopped around until a sound
Caused him to fly away.

John C. Dailey

Wedding Day

On this day, March twenty-one,
When we were wed some years ago,
Our lives forever changed, sweet doe,
Joined together then as one.

I still recall that spring-like day,
Friends and family filled the hall.
Our vows were made in front of all
Then off we went on our married way.

Shipmates

When I think back on days gone by
I sometimes pause and wonder why
It came to pass that we should be
Shipmates on the choppy sea

Of life. As strangers passing in the night
Looking first to left and then to right,
Sailing forth with charts unknown
In fragile barques, all alone

At first. But as dawn's glow replaced the night,
We both found refuge from our flight
In waters calm; our anchors dropped,
Blinking lights announced our stop

To rest. And looking fore and aft I saw
You sitting there against the wall.
I didn't know you at the time
And had to ask a friend of mine

Your name. From that moment until now,
The weather fair and sometimes foul,
Our ship has sailed most everywhere,
Guided by the special care

Of God Himself. March twenty-first, the day we wed.
Winter passed and spring came forth and said
We would be one for ever more
In nineteen hundred and sixty-four.

John C. Dailey

Anniversary Day

It's been two-score plus ten years since we wed.
We voiced our vows though I don't recall what we said.
And while time has passed for me and you,
Our life remains forever new.

.

Now my hair is thin
And I have two chins.
My girth has changed:
I've been rearranged.

But you remain sweet and fair,
Though shorter than in yesteryear.
With ruby lips and smooth soft skin,
My princess bride, let's do it all again.

While we may have changed in shape and size,
Our bond of hearts we realize
Is stronger now than in times past.
Our constant love will always last.

Commemorating Our 50th Wedding Anniversary on 3/21/2014

John C. Dailey

The Birthday Girl

Someday, dear child,
You will know,
Why it is
We love you so.

Curly blond hair
And twinkling eyes,
A smiling face
Devoid of lies.

You are God's gift,
A joy to behold.
You brighten each day
And make our lives whole.

Yes, Jane Frances, now that you're ONE,
You're our Venus at night and our morning Sun.

For Jane Frances, January 30, 2014

John C. Dailey

Fingers McCoy

She's a cute little girl
Just TWO years old,
With bright blue eyes and long blond curls,
And fingers that like to hold

On tight to anything that's in sight.
She's not very tall
In terms of her height.
And yet she can find things that are small

Or large, and she's able
To grab her treasures
From the counter or table.
Then she laughs as she measures

Her booty and runs away
To her special storage place,
Which happens to be her stroller today;
Tomorrow it may be a different space.

She's able to gather your keys
Or your wallet and change.
And of course whatever she sees
Is all fair game.

For all of her sweet rascally schemes,
This beautiful, lovable child remains
The special gift of her mother's dreams
And my beguiling granddaughter, Miss Jane.

For Jane Frances, January 30, 2015

The Three-Year-Old Cutie Pie

My grandpa says I'm a cutie pie.
My daddy says now be a good,
Jane, and we'll go bye bye
In the car. My mama thinks I should
Take a nap first 'cause I'm fussy.
But now that I am three years old
They should know I'm not a baby
Anymore. I really don't like to be told
What to do except I know if I'm bad
I might not get to play with my toys
Or read books and then I'd be sad.
What is a girl supposed to do? Play with boys?

I asked gramma and she said, no
Jane, you're too young for boys.
Just come and sit on my lap so
I can give you a hug. Don't make any noise.
See grandpa? He fell asleep in the chair
Again, watching the movie. Let me whisper
In your ear so we don't wake him. He's a bear
When he's grumpy. Don't worry, Jane. If he were
A real bear he'd be all furry. Come sit in your chair
And we'll have some birthday cake. I think you're
A cutie pie too. Now that you're THREE, take care
Dear Jane. Our love for you will forever endure.

For Jane Frances, January 30, 2016

John C. Dailey

I'm a Big Girl Now

"I'm a big girl now," she said,
The little girl with the long blond hair.
"And I have a big girl's bed,
And I go to preschool over there,"
As she pointed outside. "Where's your school?'
I asked, but she just laughed and took
My hand. "Come on, you can sit on the footstool
And we can watch a movie or read a book."
"Ok, but first you have to tell me your name."
"Oh, grandpa, you know my name, Jane Frances
Rottjakob," "And how old are you, Miss Jane?'
"I'm FOUR years old," she said with great emphasis,
As she started watching her favorite show.
I sat with her awhile and thought, will I even know
Her in a year or two? Dear Jane, as you depart
From childhood may you never lose your childhood heart.

For Jane Frances, 1/30/17

The "Big Girl" Turns Five

It seems like only yesterday, Miss Jane,
When you were four. And now dear
Child I'm here to joyfully exclaim
The news that you've turned FIVE. Another year

Has come and gone. You're taller now, a blond-
Haired lass whose sweet smile brightens
All around, like a magic wand,
Turning darkness into light.

What would I do if you had never come to be,
If you were never you? I can't imagine what I would say
Except to thank the Lord for letting me see
This special birthday girl we honor today.

For Jane Frances, 1/30/18

John C. Dailey

Sweet Six

My, my, it's time to celebrate.
Our sweet SIX-year old is another year
Older. January thirty, the day we commemorate
Your birthday once again, my dear.

"Grandpa, I really like school,"
She said as she climbed the stairs to her room.
It was bedtime for the tired birthday girl.
She donned her jammies and said her prayers. Soon

She was fast asleep. "She's growing up,"
I said, realizing she has reached a new threshold.
She's learning to read and write and develop
Her own special charm, our sweet SIX-year old.

And if you're ever sad or gloomy, dear mademoiselle,
Just say a prayer to your namesake, St. Jane Frances de Chantel.

For Jane Frances, 1/30/19

John C. Dailey

The Unicorn's Secret

So what did the Unicorn say to the Rabbit
As they walked alongside the garden wall?
Could it be about that scalawag, Bridget,
The teddy bear who threw a snowball

At Jane who was on her way to school?
Or could it be about Charlotte, that wily spider
Who frightened poor Jane when she sat on a stool
At school and the spider sat down beside her?

The Unicorn smiled and said, "No, it's not about
Bridget or Charlotte but I'll give you a clue.
It's about one day each year when you shout
Out a familiar and special song to someone who

Is one year older and wiser and more beautiful and you say,
'Jane Frances Rottjakob, Happy SEVENTH Birthday.'"

For Jane from Grandpa,
January 30, 2020

The Celebration

The Pyredoodle with the curly white coat
Introduced herself to Charlie, the shy white cat.
"Hey, I'm Daisy. I just arrived from Terre Haute.
What's your name, Mr. Cat? I'd like to have a chat.

I'm here to celebrate someone's special day,
And I hope to have some fun along the way."
"Well, my name's Charlie, and there's a party for Jane
Coming up soon. The Unicorn will help to entertain

And with grandma Pat, auntie Kate, Gab, Jack and Rose,
What a great day it'll be for everyone there.
Because it happens just once a year, everyone knows,
With family and friends, it's a swell affair."

"And Charlie, what's the event we're to celebrate?"
"Gee, Jane Frances Rottjakob has finally turned EIGHT."

For Jane from Grandpa,
January 30, 2021

John C. Dailey

The Story of the Bees

My kitty, Miss Gracie, told me she heard
Some of my bees who were buzzing about
Something that was going to happen. The word
She heard was there was some big turnout

On the horizon that would be soon, though
She couldn't remember where or when.
Since I was bitten by the blue butterfly, I know
The meaning of their buzzing so I listened again,

And this is what I heard: Queen Bee, Ellen Christine,
Told her handsome drone, named, Jim,
That a party was being planned with a go-between
Who will get everything ready, starting with the hymn,

"Happy Birthday to a special NINE year old Honey Bee,
Jane Frances Rottjakob. Hallelujah and glory be!"

*Happy Ninth Birthday, Jane,
from your Grandpa, John
January 30, 2022.*

The First Decade Girl

What is a decade? Do you know?
Is it a length of time or a deck of cards?
Is it a big red ball that you can roll?
It might be something easy or something hard.

A decade is one-half of a score,
And your rosary has five decades.
A decade of pennies is a dime, not one penny more.
So do you understand everything I have said?

On the day of your birth in 2023,
You'll be a decade old, ten years.
As we gather 'round we hope to see
Laughter and joy and singing, but no tears.

And so Jane Frances, I have one thing to say:
Happy tenth birthday on this special day.

Happy Birthday, Jane,
from your Grandpa, John
January 30, 2023

John C. Dailey

#11

There is a little girl
With light blond hair
Who lives in a big white house
With a long straight stair.

Born on a cold and wintery day,
Her mom and dad's pride and joy.
A January girl who helps light our way
On the perilous journey we call life.

As we gather together to wish her
Good cheer, we celebrate
Another year that has passed by.
It's time everyone, come on, we can't wait

To say, "Happy Birthday, Miss Jane,
Happy # 11. May you always stay the same."

Birthday wishes for Jane Frances
Rottjakob on her eleventh birthday,
January 30, 2024, from her grandpa,
John C. Dailey.

Willow's Song

Oh, Willow, sing your song for all;
We're listening to your siren call.
Your enchanting music doth enthrall,
Oh, beautiful girl with the auburn hair.

Your sunny smile, a happy tune,
Begins to play, and very soon
The sound of joy fills the room.
Oh, beguiling bairn with the auburn hair.

Oh, Willow sing your song for me
And I will sing along with thee;
And sing your song for our family.
Oh, grandchild with the auburn hair.

John C. Dailey

Philomena Grace

Philomena Grace, beloved infant child
Of the lovely Lady Amanda and learned Sir Sean,
Welcome to the O'Dalaigh Clan. Your undefiled
Body and soul are truly a gift from God. Born

In the winter of twenty-two 'midst a world gone
Mad, you are a shining light of peace and delight.
Your sister and brothers, Rose, Gabriel and John,
Your friends forever, will help direct you in the fight

To find justice and truth. You will lead the way and be
A beacon of light, guiding all who seek eternal life.
Most favored by the Mystical Rose, you'll be like a bee,
And will gather the Rose's ambrosia and end all strife.

Rest easy now little one for your time is somewhere ahead.
For like St. George, the Dragon of Lies you'll someday behead.

*A sonnet celebrating the birth of Philomena Grace Dailey,
the great granddaughter of John and Pat Dailey,
January 26. 2022*

Rose's First Birthday

It's difficult sometimes
To know just what to say,
Dear Rose, to someone who
Is celebrating her FIRST birthday.

Unless, that is, unless that
Someone is someone like you, a lovely
Irish lass who, by your birth, has united
The Clans, (O) Brennan and (O) Daly.

So therefore on this happy day
I honor you, my great granddaughter.
My wish for you is good health, a long life,
And the strength of the mountains of Ballyhoura.

For Rose Catherine Dailey, 2/24/18

John C. Dailey

Growing Up
(A Mother's Prayer for Her Son)

When you were just a babe and I held you in my arms,
I rocked you gently back and forth and prayed no harm
Would come your way; and when you cried I lifted you
Up onto my lap and brushed away your tears. And true
To form, your crying stopped and, oh yes, I remember how
You smiled and sighed sweet sounds, and I would bow
My head and rub my forehead on your nose. You giggled
As you pulled my hair and I tried to pull away but you wiggled
Back and forth and I finally had to put you down and catch my breath.

It seems like overnight and it was time for you to go to school.
Tears filled my eyes as I watched you go. I must have been a fool
To think that you would never leave; that you would never grow
Into a man, that my baby boy would someday have to show
The world that he is smart and tough and strong of will.
I weep within, knowing all the pain you have suffered and must suffer still
As you move on in life and seek the goal that's in your heart.
You're older now and yet you are so very young. As you start
Your quest, please know that I am with you every day.

Ode to a Seven-Year-Old Boy

I know a seven-year old boy
Who makes my heart sing with joy.
He likes to climb on rocks and trees
And fly kites in the summer breeze.

Youth is such a transient thing,
Passing quietly like the spring
Into the days of older age,
Ending in the wise old sage.

Enjoy your youth; enjoy this time
When you can run and jump and climb
The pine trees in your grandpa's field
And ask the pond her fish to yield.

On this day when you are seven,
I wish you all the happiness that heaven
Can bestow on you, but wait,
For soon you will be turning eight.

John C. Dailey

A Sixteenth Birthday Wish

Once again I am drawn
To the birth of my grandson, Sean.
On February twenty-seven
We received a gift from heaven.
Nineteen ninety-two in fact
Was the year to be exact.

The memory of that happy day
When you were born began to play
Upon my brain, and I began
To ask the question once again
What if you had never come to be?
What if God had never let us see

Your tiny body born, so frail?
But when we heard your lusty wail
All our fears, like wisps of mist, were gone.
We laughed and cried and burst into a song
Of joy. But then our fears returned.
Your breathing stopped. We never learned

The reason why, but you revived.
Through God's great mercy you survived.
That tiny babe, all blond and fair,
Is growing up. And where
He used to cry and be afraid,
He now stands tall and strong and staid.

And I will keep a promise made
To love you forever, and wade
Through all life's trials by your side
Until I can go no more. The tide
Will roll in to bear me away.
And when it happens, on that day

You'll be fine to carry on
Even though I'll be gone.
Your Father in heaven will watch where you run
For you are his very special son.
And I'll be there too
Always watching over you.

John C. Dailey

The Lost Child

There is sadness in my heart
And soul, and in every body part.
Like a dreary day with clouds and rain,
There was no brightness, only darkness came.
If I were able, I would scream
"Why has this happened, this terrible dream,
This nightmare that will not end:
My son is gone; his mother weeps; who will mend
Her broken heart and dry her tears?"
Alas, we're at a loss; what should we do? We fear
That we may never see his face again.
He left without a word. And when
We found out he had gone it was too late
To say good-bye. Why wouldn't he wait
And tell us what was on his mind?
He even left his wife and kids behind.

Now years have passed and still no word
From him has come. It's like a sword
Has pierced our hearts and our family's
Life now oozes forth, a bloody sea
Of sorrow. Will our lives ever be the same again?

Happiness

Happiness is a simple thing,
Yet sometimes so hard to find.
For we always look to the things of the world,
But the things of the world have no mind.

As a child l laughed and played silly games
And drew pictures with crayons and chalk.
l passed each day in a simple way
And found joy where'er l would walk.

Now as a man l no longer play games,
Yet l still find joy in a simple place,
From the dip of my paddle in an eventide lake,
To your laughing eyes and your smiling face.

To you then l say in my simple way,
"Te amo, Dios te ama and Happy Birthday."

John C. Dailey

A Birthday Wish

So, another year has passed
And once again your birthday is here.
After all these years have you really changed that much?
Your beauty is still the same, my dear.
You know that l will always be your special friend,
For time will never erase what is so clear;
You are my sun and moon and stars.

The End of Summer

lt was one of those special September days
As l sat on my back porch. Please,
You know what l mean...the way
The autumn leaves sway gently in the breeze,

And tiny humming birds slip by so fast
l almost miss seeing them at their feeders, and our
Beautiful roses are still showing off their last
Blooms, and butterflies are darting from flower to flower.

A peacefulness pervades all around, mirrored
By the occasional music of the chimes on the patio.
lt's a good feeling to be here, a torch bearer
Of the present and yet l'm sad for l know

That things will change in a few weeks time
As the world transitions to a new paradigm.

A Sonnet for Patricia Ann

In the second month of every year
Two days of some moment occur
That I cannot forget. And if it happened that I did,
Oh my, I'd be one mournful kid.

Both days combined are thirty one
And each alone less than nineteen. But for some
To guess what they are may seem
What Cervantes has called "...an impossible dream..."

For someone like you and your supercharged brain
The deductive process should not be a strain.
Saints Cyril and Methodius are already there
And the Servite Founders contribute their share.

So have you by now determined the days?
Or is the solution still a foggy maze?

John C. Dailey

A Birthday Wish for Pat

Oh, my, it's birthday time again.
I thought I'd seen the celebrations end when
We had Christmas and the New Year feast
Then Valentine's to say the least.

But birthdays are a special time
When we can bring forth words that rhyme
And realize, as I've been told,
They mean much more than growing old.

Your birthday means that you've been born,
Your first breath taken on a February morn
In the year when our country went to war
To preserve our freedom for ever more.

And so without further ado, let me say,
"I love you, Pat, and Happy Birthday."

A Sonnet for Ellen

Just forty-seven years ago
To Riverside we all did go.
Your birth brought everyone such joy
When they said, "It's a girl, not a boy."

The years since then have quickly passed.
You're all grown up and have cast
Off on your ship of life:
A beautiful lady, mother and wife.

And so, on this April seventeen
In the year two thousand fifteen,
Mom and I just want to say:
Dear Ellen, "Have a Very Happy Birthday."

If these words should be found untrue
Then there is no sun nor sky of blue.

John C. Dailey

Edith and Isla*

Grandchildren and Great Grandchildren are truly gifts
From God. Born from the love of their mother
and dad, they bring happiness and certitude in a world bereft
Of sanity. We are so excited to express our delight that another

Child is born. Edith Josephine and Isla Skye are sweet
Baby girls, protected by Our Mother Most Admirable,
And loved without reservation by all. Our life is complete
That they're here and safe, in a world that wants to kill

Babies before they're born. Oh, Lord, how long can You afford
The slaughter of the unborn, the killing of the innocents,
Before you destroy the killers in their killing crypts
And smite them to hell with your terrible swift sword?

Dedicated to our two new Great Granddaughters,
Edith Josephine Sadaj, 9/30/21,
and Isla Skye DeSena, 3/30/22.

*Isla is pronounced,"Ila"

Mable Christine Presson Bean
on Her Eightieth Birthday

Three score and twenty years long past
In sunny Tennessee down south,
November seventh came at last
And the Pressons added one more mouth.

The Presson Clan was, Oh so proud,
A girl to go with Tommy boy.
To find a name they asked a crowd
Of family friends who shared their joy.

Sitting by the fireside bright
Drinking steins of Black Label brew,
They called for more all day and night
And picked a name both bold and true.

"Hey Mabel, Black Label," they called out loud.
And Gussie said, "That's all for a while;
Mabel's a name that will make her proud
And we'll add Christine to give her some style."

The years passed by and the family moved
To live in old St. Louis town
Where she and Mr. Ted Bean grooved
And wedding bells began to sound.

Before very long the family grew,
Along with lots of joy and some misery.
First Teddy then Pat then Peggy Lou,
And many grandchildren soon to be.

That brings us to the present time.
And I'd like to wish this gal the best.
I'll call it quits and end this rhyme
Saying "Happy Birthday" with all the rest.

John C. Dailey

To a Priest of St. Ignatius on His Seventieth Birthday

Now come we all to speak the truth
About a man of faith. In sooth,
Known to those assembled here,
From his devout life it is clear

This is a man of God,
A priest, ordained to trod
The footsteps of the soldier-priest of Spain,
Reciting the ancient Ignatian strain:

"Anima Christi, sanctifica me.
Ne permittas me separari a te."
"Soul of Christ, sanctify me.
Permit me not to be separated from thee."

To Father Baker these words are said.
Three-score and ten years past, and more ahead.

For Fr. Kenneth Baker, SJ, November 11, 1999.

My Nurse

I was pretty sick last year;
Spent a month in the hospital.
I don't think I'd still be here,
Except for my nurse, Miss Kathleen.

Fell asleep while smoking in bed;
What a dumb thing to do.
I should have known better, she said,
My nurse, Miss Kathleen.

The burn unit was a busy place;
I don't remember much except
She was always there on my case,
My nurse, Miss Kathleen.

I know I'll never forget her
And the loving care she gave.
My time on the unit is still a blur,
Except for my nurse, Miss Kathleen.

For my daughter, Kathleen, nurse extraordinaire.

John C. Dailey

The Christmas Visitors

One of my fondest memories of days long ago
Is when my cousins and aunt and uncle came
To visit us for Christmas. They traveled by rail so
We had to get up very early to meet their train,

Which arrived before dawn. I still remember standing
By the tracks, the cold winter air numbing my face.
It was hard to contain my excitement, holding
Mothers hand, when I heard the first trace

Of the train, the sound of the whistle in the distance.
It seemed like forever before the whistle sounded once more
And I could hear the din of the wheels pounding in cadence,
Clickety-clack, clickety-clack, and then a giant man-of-war

Came into view and stopped a few feet away in the cold winter
Air. The black locomotive was enormous, like a huge Bessemer
Converter, billowing smoke and steam, catching its breath before
Moving on. From a long string of passenger cars, all aglimmer

With lights penetrating the darkness outside, a few people deboarded.
Pretty soon I saw Chuck and Jim , Uncle Peter and Aunt Bernice.
We exchanged hugs and kisses and took their luggage and loaded
Up our car and headed home for Christmas in the early dawn's greyness.

John C. Dailey

Christmas Eve

I remember, many years ago,
When I was young and still believed
In Santa Clause, our family would go
To mass on Christmas Eve,
And hurry home for the traditional dinner
Of mom's special clam chowder. Then we gathered 'round
The Christmas tree to decorate it. We were
So excited: Santa, the twinkling lights, the sound
Of *Silent Night*, and then to bed, to wait
Impatiently for the night visitor,
Hoping he wouldn't forget the bike and ice skates.
I don't think I ever fell asleep, the clam chowder
Roiling around inside of me. And when I opened my eyes
At first light it was as if it was all a dream,
Until I heard my little brother calling me; his excited cries
Of wonder and surprise finally woke me up. The gleam
Of lights and the toys by the tree were more than enough proof
For us to see that Santa had been there. Anticipation
Had given way to the joy that he was not an imaginary spoof
But something real that we could believe in. Emancipation
From the innocence of childhood often changes our outlook
On life and clouds those precious memories of times past.

Mother's Day

What do we mean by Mother's Day?
Is it a day when we might say
Nice things about a special lady
Who is always there to get us ready
For school or work, who mends
Our clothes and fixes us meals and sends
Us on our way into the world? Yes, but it must
Be more than that. It is a day to honor the one we trust
Will always be there, whether mother or wife,
Whose whole role in life is to give her life
For us. Surely, one day is really not enough to honor her.

John C. Dailey

Part Two
Love and Romance

Part Two Contents

Introduction: Love and Romance

This is a collection of poems that are more recent, all written within the last ten years. The poems about friendship, roses, and Venus are presented with alternate versions of the same theme. The shorter version of "Morning Star, Evening Star" was previously published in the magazine, *Ireland of the Welcomes*. The poems about love were inspired by my muse, especially the last poem in the group, "The Ballad of the Lady and the Knight," which takes place in Ireland In the late middle ages.

> "Let me not to the marriage of true minds
> Admit impediments; love is not love
> Which alters when it alteration finds,
> Or bends with the remover to remove:
> O, no! it is an ever-fixed mark,
> That looks on tempests and is never shaken."
>
> —Shakespeare, from *Sonnet 110*

What Is Love?

I've had this funny feeling
For at least a month or two.
My heart beats fast, can't sleep at night
Whenever I am close to you.

At first I wasn't sure just why,
You've been around so long.
Then I found I felt that way
Whenever you were gone.

Then sitting at your desk one day
I looked into your drawer.
And there beside some paper clips
I heard a quiet rumbling roar.

I quickly pushed it closed
And looked the other way.
Had anyone around me heard
The sound I heard that day?

Well, no one seemed to notice
And you were not around.
So I opened up the drawer again
And listened to the sound.

Yes, the paper clips seemed to be
The source of that strange sound.
I gently moved them to the side
And guess what then I found?

John C. Dailey

A tiny vial of golden fluid,
The source of that soft lilting whine.
And written on the label was,
"Love Potion Number Nine."

The vial was almost empty
But still I heard that sound.
So I picked it up and popped the cork
And poured it on the ground.

I bet that's why I've felt so strange.
You put the potion on your lips and skin.
Then when we kissed and hugged and kissed
The potion's power would always win.

On second thought that can't be true.
The potions gone, been thrown away.
Yet now that feeling still persists.
I need you more and more each day.

Do you believe in love potions?
I don't think I do.
I do believe what's in my heart
And what's in my heart is you

Do You Love Me?

"Dear Sean, do you love me?"
"Oh yes, Amanda, I love you."
"But how do I know, how can it be?"
"Amanda, it's not something I say or do.
No, my love for you is like a fire
Within my soul. When e'er I even think of you
The flame flares higher and higher
And I am consumed by you, my Love so true."

"Dear Sean, do you know I love you?"
"Oh yes, Amanda, I know you love me"
"But do you know how much I love you?
Do you know that you are actually
The essence of the air I breathe,
The sun that shines by day, the moon and stars
That light my way at night. My soul does not deceive:
It is alive and yearns for you whether near or far."

For the newlyweds, 6/3/16.

John C. Dailey

Love Actually

As we begin this festive Season
I'd like to let you know the reason
Why I need you near to me
As we journey on this bumpy sea
Of life. You know you are my special friend,
For whom my love will never end.
Your beauty and your grace abound
More than you can ever know. So when I sound
My call to you to come and sit down by my side
And listen to the whirling wind as we ride
On misty clouds of hopes and dreams,
Know that things aren't always what they seem.
Remember love is an emotion that we feel
Inside. Passion first, then knowing that real
Love can only be a spiritual sensation
Within one's heart and soul, the realization
That true love is when we seek each other's heart
And know that we can never ever part.

Love's Lament

When I am with you
My whole being is at peace.
Without you, sadness.

Friendship

You must know my friend, I think
about you every day.

My love for you is as constant as the
rising and the setting of the sun.

And nothing you can do will ever change
what now I say:

The flame that lights my soul will vanish
when your day is done.

John C. Dailey

My Friend

Each night when I retire to bed,
I think of you, my dearest friend.
For it is you that I desire. Let it be said,
My quest for you will never end.

Remembering your soft caress, I sought
To keep your vision bright.
Your beauty fills my every thought
As I dream onward through the night.

Your perfect form brings me delight,
Your skin so smooth and soft.
Your soulful shining eyes so bright
Have taken me to heights aloft.

The air is very thin up here
But I am not afraid, my friend.
I see you standing very near,
Your smile my guide unto the end.

Mystical Muse

Oh mystical muse, I called your name,
As I lay dreaming by the shore.
My thoughts are always just the same:
My love for you now and ever more.

Where are you dear lady, are you nearby?
I cannot see your laughing smile,
Nor can I hear your soothing sigh.
Please, come and stay with me awhile.

Ah, I think I hear you calling me.
Yes, I'm sure that's your voice, so clear.
Come closer now so I may see
Your beauty beaming far and near.

For you are unique in all the world,
A gentle woman blessed by the Lord.

John C. Dailey

An Apology

Oh Friend, I've said some things I'm sorry for
And now you must be feeling all alone.
For you, dear Friend, have faith and love of more
Worth than any coin or precious stone.

How could I have been so cruel,
So self-righteous and oblique?
Is it because I'm just a fool,
A man whose faith and love are weak?

I pray thee, Lord, be my guide
As I traverse this arduous path
Of asking for forgiveness. Abide
In me should I suffer my Friend's wrath.

Oh, Friend, I beg thee, ease my soul's pain.
Your reprieve will bring me peace again.

John C. Dailey

How Cometh the Rose

When I look upon a rose,
I wonder how it came to be
That God, Our Lord, who knows
All things, created so much beauty.

Then I looked into your eyes
And knew how it came to be.
God's model, it is no surprise
Was you, dear love, it's plain to see.

Your velvet skin so soft and smooth,
Your subtle scent from heaven above,
These traits that are your essence prove
You are God's mold, the object of His Love.

Ponder these thoughts within your heart
For they are true beyond all doubt.

The Rose

When I gaze upon a rose
I wonder how it came to be
That God, Our Lord, who knows
All things, created such beauty for all to see?

Then I looked into your eyes
And found the answer that I sought.
God's model, it was no surprise
Was you, my love, from heaven wrought.

You reflect the rose in every way.
Your eyes so bright and full of love
Like the colors of the buds that say
"We are beautiful blooms from heaven above."

Your velvet skin so smooth and soft
Like the petals of each flower,
And a sweet subtle scent that wafts aloft
From you, dear muse, in your ivory tower.

Though I may never pluck this bloom
And place her in my vase,
I will love her forever; and whom
Ever doubts will disappear without a trace.

John C. Dailey

Morning Star, Evening Star

Viewing the eastern heavenly scene
One morning before dawn
I saw a bright and twinkling gleam
Amid the pink and yellow glow of morn.

For it was you I saw, oh Morning Star,
My celestial guide and friend.
I marveled at your beauty from afar
And prayed the vision wouldn't end.

You're always there my love, my dear,
Shining bright for all to see.
Whether cloudy sky or bright and clear,
I know that's where you'll always be.

Now eventide has come once more;
The light is fading in the west.
Looking up, I watch you as you soar,
Dancing there, doing what you do best.

Oh Evening Star, I love you so.
I long to fold my arms around your waist
And bathe within the brightness of your glow.
But I am here on earth and you are far away in space.

I pray our paths will cross one day,
And I'll reach out and draw you near.
Your light will brighten up the way
And give me strength and calm my fear.

Morning Star, Evening Star #2

I saw a dazzling, twinkling glow
Amid the pink and yellow light of dawn,
A faithful sentinel showing where to go.
Oh Morning Star, be it land or sea
You're always there my love,
Shining bright for all to see.

The light is fading in the west.
Looking up, I see you once again,
Dancing there, doing what you do best.
Oh Evening Star, I love you so.
I long to fold my arms around your waist
And bathe within the brightness of your glow.

John C. Dailey

Miss Grace

The Ballad of
the Lady
and the Knight

John C. Dailey

I

She dwelled on top a mountain peak, the lovely Lady
　　Eveleen.
He lived down in the Village below, on the other side
　　of a deep ravine.
He saw her one day in the Village Square and asked his
　　man, Will,
"Who is that maid with the bright blue eyes and auburn
　　hair that makes my heart stand still?"
"Alas, Sir Sean, that's the Lady Eveleen from the
　　mountain peak who has drawn your gaze.
But rest your sword and rein in your steed; don't look
　　too long or spend many days
Thinking of her. For you see she's betrothed to a
　　fearsome Knight,
Lord Brian de Lough, who guards his lair and all within
　　and would fight
To the death any man or beast if he thinks they might
　　steal away
His Lady Eveleen. And yet I have heard he grows weary
　　of her; some say
She is sad and alone in her castle while he travels about
　　to the jousting events.
Her family is gone and she longs to be loved but he's nev-
　　er there. He sent
Her a gift for her bedroom floor, the skin of a cat, that he
　　felled one day;
But it made her cry for it looked like her kitty, Miss
　　Grace, who ran away with a stray."

II

"I fear no man or beast," said Sir Sean as he listened to the tale
Will told. "I have fallen in love with Lady Eveleen and I'll not fail
To make her my bride." Will pondered his words then looked up
    and said,
"My liege, you're not free to seek a spouse. Remember, though
    you would like to wed,
Your aging mother needs you still. And though your bed be
    empty and cold,
You are bound to protect her as she grows old."
"Yes, friend Will, I know what you say, and I'll not fail to fulfill
    my task
And give her shelter and care until her last dying breath. But to
    you I ask:
How do I deal with the passion I feel in my heart and soul?
Do I simply ignore it and hope that in time it will pass?
    My whole
Life may be gone before that day. Oh Lord, let me not time
    waste
To bring Lady Eveleen to my side. If I could only find her kitty,
    Miss Grace,
I feel I would win her heart and her love. Yes, Will, that will be
    my quest:
To find her lost cat and bring her home; until she is found I will
    not rest."

John C. Dailey

III

And so Sir Sean and his faithful friend, Will, went to his
    castle, Glensheen,
Where they gathered their men and made plans. "Has anyone
    seen
That cat?" Sir Sean asked. "Does anyone know where it could
    have gone?"
One of the men said he heard a meow from the ravine and a
    maidservant, Fiona McBraun,
Daughter of Kevin McBraun, remembered seeing a large
    brown cat in the ravine.
She said it had a red ribbon around its neck like Miss Grace
    when she was last seen.
"Then mount up my men and we'll find that cat; but how shall
    we catch it when she is found?"
Fiona McBraun spoke up again and said, "Sir Sean, you must
    take ten pounds
Of Mighty Bowl Litter, the kind that Miss Grace can't resist.
    It's said she loves to spend
Time in that dirty grey clay relieving herself. Lady Eveleen
    has to send
A wagon each month to the village to haul thirty bags on the
    trail
Back to her castle, Fairview." With that Sir Sean shouted,
    "Then we are off and we shall not fail."
As he mounted his stallion, Ronan, Will and the others
    mounted up as well and
Will filled his bags with the grey-colored litter. "We'll find that
    cat even if by sleight of hand."

IV

As they followed the trail into the ravine, Will asked Sir Sean,
    "My Lord how do you know
That Lady Eveleen will return your love if you find her cat?
    Do you have any sign to show
That she feels about you as you feel about her?" Sir Sean
    paused and looked at Will
And said, "I feel her heart in my heart, our two hearts
    beating as one. When it is very still
I can hear her voice calling to me, telling of her love. I know
    that somehow, somewhere,
Someday we will meet, for I have no doubt that her love is
    there.
I know she cares for me even though we may never be wed.
    I am not worthy to hold
This beautiful maid's hand, and yet our Blessed Lord has
    brought us together. I have told
You enough, Will. We must be on our way for it will soon be
    dark."
And so the troupe moved slowly down the ravine into the
    forest.
    A meadowlark
Called in the distance. The last light of day faded as they set
    up camp by a stream.
Sir Sean and Will sat by the campfire drinking mead. A
    moonbeam
Filtered through the trees, the sounds of the night in the
    background.
Soon all were asleep, the silence broken only by their soft
    snoring sound.

John C. Dailey

V

They were up at dawn to begin their pursuit of Miss Grace,
    the missing feline.
Sir Sean reminded the men of the plan of how that elusive cat
    they would find:
"We'll put the litter along the trail and hide nearby until she
    appears; then a net
Will be thrown while she squats in the litter to piddle and
    poop. Once the trap is set
She'll not escape. We'll drop her into a large cloth bag and I'll
    travel with haste
To Fairview where Lady Eveleen waits patiently for her re-
    turn. I'll not waste
One minute to bring Miss Grace home. I pray
It is not too late for I know Lady Eveleen's heart grows sad-
    der each day that her cat is away."
By midday the cat was not yet caught so the men decided to
    lead her astray.
Kevin McBraun suggested they use his pet cat, Muirne.
"We'll place a collar round her neck and stake her by the
    trail," he said,
"And when Miss Grace hears her meowing, she'll be led
By the sound to the pile of litter. She will be no match for this
    ruse.
She will soon be ours and Sir Sean can return her home with
    nary a bruise."

VI

The trap was set. Sir Sean leaned against an old oak tree
And closed his eyes and dreamed about how life would be
If he could only hold Lady Eveleen in his arms and kiss her
    sweet lips.
His dream suddenly ceased when he heard someone yell,
    "Eureka! She'll not give us the slip,
We've caught that wily cat." He jumped up and looked around
To see from whence the sound had come. Down the trail on
    the ground
He saw his men holding a bag and shouting, "We've got her,
    Sir Sean."
Sir Sean took Ronan's reins and first led him up the trail to a
    pond
Where he let him drink; then he climbed in the saddle
And went back down the trail toward his men. The trail was
    so narrow that he had to straddle
The edge lest he and Ronan fall off into a ditch. Kevin Mc-
    Braun gave him the bag.
"God speed, Sir Sean, as you finish your quest. Take care for I
    saw a large stag
Bounding off through the woods. His rack is big and his horns
    are keen.
Take the river trail to Fairview. You'll be safe and will not be
    seen."

John C. Dailey

VII

Sir Sean tied the bag to his saddle and sang to Miss Grace
    as he moved along.
He sang of two people and of love that may never be, a
    sad song
Indeed, that made him grieve as he followed the trail to his
    true love's abode.
Soon he saw the towers of Fairview rising up down the road.
He stopped for a while and opened the bag and held Miss
    Grace close to his chest.
"Don't be afraid my little cat friend. You'll soon be home to
    your little cat nest.
Lady Eveleen will be happy again and my quest will be done.
I'll return to my village with a new found friend but will I
    have won
Her love? If she could but say what I want to hear,
That she'll love me forever even though I'm not near,
Then my soul will find peace at last and I'll know
That my quest for her love wasn't in vain. I'll stroll
Down the trail a most happy Knight.
I've won my love's heart and have fought the good fight."

John C. Dailey

VIII

Sir Sean put Miss Grace back into the bag
And rode on to Fairview. His shoulders began to sag
As he drew closer. He worried that when he returned her cat
He might never see Lady Eveleen again. When he arrived at
    last, he doffed his hat
To a young lady standing by the front door. "Hello, good Sir,"
    she said. "I'm
Brianna Delaney, Lady Eveleen's maidservant. Rest yourself
    and take some time
From your journey. How may I be of service?" Sir Sean dis-
    mounted and handed over
The bag to Brianna. "This is Lady Eveleen's wayward cat,
    Miss Grace. The little rover
Was is the ravine running with a stray but she seems fine.
We gave her some food and cleaned her up. She looks a bit
    thin but in time
She'll be well." Brianna smiled and held Miss Grace in her lap.
    "I would
Hope this will ease my Lady's distress. Ever since Lord Brian
    trod
Off to seek his fortune, vowing not to return, she has been in
    pain. Kind Sir,
Would you please come into the castle and meet her?"

IX

"If it would not be upsetting to her I would be honored to greet
Her. I am Sir Sean of the Clan O'Barrett. When I saw her sweet
Face in the village market place I fell in love and made a vow
To devote my life to her. That is why when I was told of Miss Grace's meow
In the ravine and how sad my dear Lady was that her cat had run off,
I set out with my men to find her and bring her home. I did not scoff
At what seemed an impossible task." Sir Sean then nodded to Brianna
And followed her. They entered a large room which looked out upon a vast savanna.
A stone fireplace was at one end of the room, much like the one in his castle,
Glensheen. Lady Eveleen sat on a couch by the fire. She was bashful
At first. Brianna introduced Sir Sean and placed Miss Grace in her arms.
"I am so grateful, Sir Sean, to have Miss Grace back again, safe and unharmed.
I cannot thank you enough. Please come and sit next to me and hold my hand.
Oh gallant Knight, some pain still remains. Lord Brian has left me alone in this lonely land."

John C. Dailey

X

"He said he was leaving to seek his fortune but I doubt that's
   really the case.
My Scribe, Dame Sorcha Blake, is also gone and I fear she has
   taken my place
In his heart. He has always had a wandering eye but I never
   thought he would find
Dame Sorcha more appealing. She's more buxom than me and
   her morals remind
Me of an uncouth wench." Sir Sean looked at her beautiful blue
   eyes and saw her sadness.
He told her how he has fallen in love with her that day in the
   village. "Forgive my brashness
But my life has not been the same since then. Be not con-
   cerned by Lord Brian's leaving.
I will protect you. I have pledged my life to you. Do not be
   grieving
For him. As a sign of my fidelity to you, please wear this chain
   of emeralds and gold
And know that you are in my heart and mind. Before I grow old
I will take you to Glensheen as my own. Meanwhile you must
   stay here
In Fairview and wait for the time when we can consummate
   our love. Have no fear:
I am with you always. A further sign of my love and commit-
   ment to you,
Lady Eveleen, will be given to you soon, a unique symbol of
   our love so true."

XI

She took his hand and held him close, then kissed his cheek
    and said,
"Sir Sean, I accept your pledge of love and in turn I pledge my
    love to you. My bed
Will be yours when the time is right and we can be wed. Your
    being here gives me courage
And eases the pain of Lord Brian's loss." Sir Sean kissed her
    hand and fixed her image
In his mind. He stood up to take his leave and she followed
    him to the door.
He paused for a moment. The thought of leaving her was
    almost more
Than he could bear. "I bid you goodbye, dear Lady for a brief
    time. Now
That you are alone, I will send some of my men to guard you
    lest some foul
Play comes your way. Meanwhile I return to my mother,
    Lady Anne,
For she will wish to share my joy. Though advanced in years,
    she will help plan
Our wedding at the parish church in the Village. Gather your
    trousseau
And I will return in a fortnight to take you to Glensheen. One
    thing you must know:
I have joy in my heart to have found you, my true love, after
    so many years.
And though we must wait for each other now, the time will
    pass quickly, have no fear."

John C. Dailey

XII

And so Sir Sean mounted his horse and returned to
    Glensheen,
Leaving behind Lady Eveleen, sad yet full of joy. He had seen
His life pass before him, an empty life up to now, but no more.
His friend Will was waiting for him along the road. "I won't
    ignore
Lady Anne; I must hasten to Glensheen and share the news
Of my betrothal to Lady Eveleen. I'll take care and choose
My words well so as not to alarm her. Gather your men, Will.
    Send
Some to the Village with the good news and you to Fairview
    to attend
To Lady Eveleen. You are my truest friend, Will. I trust you to
    protect
Her and keep her safe until I return for her. You can help her
    collect
Her belongings. She has no family save for her maidservant,
    Brianna, and her
Kitty, Miss Grace. It will be a busy time for both of us but
    after
All we have been through together, I could not have foreseen
The gift I have been given by our Lord: my beautiful bride-to-
    be, Lady Eveleen."

XIII

When Sir Sean arrived back at Glensheen he went
To Lady Anne and hugged her and said how much it meant
To him to have her blessing for his marriage to Lady
Eveleen. Lady Anne kissed his forehead and unexpectedly
Started crying. "I am so filled with happiness for you, my son,
That I weep tears of joy for you and your betrothed. You have
    won
My blessing and more. With this marriage you will inherit
Your long-dead father's title, King of the Clan O'Barrett.
I was fearful that you might never find true love and take your
    rightful
Place as our leader. Your father's brother, Lord Gabrial,
Has threatened to take the title for himself but that will not
Be possible now. You must guard yourself against any plot
To deprive you of your birthright. I will prepare for our new
    Queen
While you return to Fairview and bring your lady to Glensheen."

John C. Dailey

XIV

Sir Sean made preparations to return to Fairview
The very next day. The thought of becoming the new
King of the Clan was overwhelming. But with Lady
Eveleen by his side he knew he'd survive. She
Would be his muse, his guiding light. Inspired by thoughts
Of his true love, Sir Sean and his troupe set off. They brought
Along a horse for Lady Eveleen, Donal, a white-faced bay
     with four
White socks, a stable-mate of Ronan, Sir Sean's horse. Before
Long they arrived at Fairview. Sir Sean's heart quickened
As he embraced his future bride. Will and his men had taken
Charge to help Brianna pack Lady Eveleen's things, and after
     resting
For two days, they were ready to return to Glensheen.
     Caressing
Miss Grace on her lap, Lady Eveleen, the future Queen and
     wife
Was seated on Donal, as she and Sir Sean rode off to their
     new life.

Part Three
People, Places, and Things

John C. Dailey

Part Three Contents

Introduction: People, Places, and Things

This group of poems features some of my favorite people. Unfortunately most of them have all gone to their reward. You will meet my Siberian cat, Miss Gracie, and journey with me to the beautiful roadless wilderness area of the BWCA and the Quetico Provincial Park. Flowers are important in our world and I feature some here. You'll also meet an Irish Legend, the Seanchai.

"If we are not able to serve man, how can we serve spiritual beings?...If we do not yet know about life how can we know about death?"

—Confucius, Analects Ch. II, v. II

"All places that the eye of heaven visits are to a wise man ports and happy havens."

—Shakespeare, Richard II (1595), act I.

The Country Doctor

My first memory of my dad was when
He was in the Army. I didn't know then
That he was a doctor who would become
A man dedicated to his patients and would overcome
Much adversity in his career. Iowa born and raised,
Imbued with a deep love of God, he blazed
His way on the long and arduous path
Of a solo rural medical practice. He suffered the wrath
Of some, who questioned his ability,
With equanimity, courage and humility.
His patients loved him because he
Was the consummate country doctor. We
Didn't see a lot of him at home; he calmly
Worked night and day, delivering a baby
Or seeing patients in the office or making
House calls or doing surgery. Taking
Time off was hard for him. Who would
Care for the folks in his absence? He understood
What it meant to be a real doctor. For all his faults,
And he had some, he never was one to exalt
Himself. If anything he was forever insecure
About his ability. And if he was unsure
What to do, he would call someone for advice.
He finally stopped smoking in the fifties, his only real vice,
But the damage to his heart was beyond repair.
His early death at seventy was a sad affair,
And yet he's not far away. He's here at my side
Whenever I care for a patient, my constant guide.

Paul A. Dailey, MD, 1908 — 1978

John C. Dailey

A Ballad for Bill Marra

Bill Marra died; he's gone to rest.
He fought the fight and passed the test.
I'm grieving now with all the rest.
We'll pray for you, Bill Marra.

When first we met at Lambert Field
His countenance was thus revealed.
A smiling face our friendship sealed.
Hello my friend, Bill Marra.

An open shirt with baggy pants,
Casual cloths meant to enhance
The shuffling, unassuming stance.
We're glad you're here, Bill Marra.

His bearded face and twinkling eyes
Provided him a fine disguise
To thwart dissenters by surprise.
We'll miss you so, Bill Marra.

For underneath that plain façade
There dwelt a mighty will that trod
Upon the enemies of God.
We need your strength, Bill Marra.

St. Augustine and von Hildebrand
Helped him to make a stand
To fight the evil in the land.
Fight for the Faith, Bill Marra.

God's faithful warrior's fate was sealed.
No coat of mail nor sword nor shield,
The lecture hall his battlefield.
We need you now, Bill Marra.

Standing there before the crowd,
Telling us we should be proud
To shout the truths of Faith out loud.
Please tell us more, Bill Marra.

To some of us it seems to me
A father he did come to be;
"Don Primo" helped us all to see.
We love you so, Bill Marra.

A guiding light, a sentinel man
Who demonstrated how we can
Be faithful to the Lord, our Lamb.
Don't leave us now, Bill Marra.

He stood for truth and righteousness.
One man against the awful stress
Of Satan's power to cause duress.
Goodbye my friend, Bill Marra.

Bill Marra's dead but he'll not rest.
He's helping us to pass the test
To gain our own eternal rest.
Thanks for your prayers, Bill Marra.

*In memory of Dr. William A. Marra,
1928 – 1998, Professor of Philosophy
at Fordham University for forty years.*

John C. Dailey

The Lecturer*

"I'm sorry but I can't let you in,
You don't have an entry ticket, my friend."
"Please, Father, give me a chance
To hear the words of this man of romance."

"You can't have a seat if you don't have a pass.
Without a ticket you can't take this class."
"Please, Father, I've waited all day by the entrance door;
I don't even care if I sit on the floor."

"I wish I could help you out, yes I do,
But I don't make the rules and neither do you."
"Please, Father, can't you bend the rule and look away
And let a poor student hear his words today?"

"Yes, I'm sure his words are most profound,
For truth in words is seldom found."
"Please, Father, since you agree,
If you let me pass, in your debt I will be."

"Why should I allow you into Washington Hall
Where he will lecture to one and all?"
"Please, Father, I beg you again;
Let me pass thru, let me in."

"Do you know who it is who is going to speak?
Do you know the person of whom you seek?"
"Please, Father, I know the name of this famous one:
He is Mr. G.K. Chesterton."

*from a talk given at the American Chesterton Society, June 14, 2014,
commemorating the series of lectures by G.K. Chesterton
at the University of Notre Dame, October-November, 1930*

A Generous Man

I knew a generous man.
He passed away last week.
We never said goodbye, just ran
Out of time I guess. Never one to seek
Fame, a soft-spoken man. But beneath his quiet
Demeanor, a steel-like strength
Prevailed, compelling him to fight
For the Faith, for life, for truth, and drink
The bitter wine of defeat, though never to concede.
He was always there for those in need.

I attended his wake. A thousand souls
Or more paid their respects; for some, their
First hello and last goodbye. The line was slow
And long. Will it never end? Yet it's only fair
To him who gave so much that we should
Wait, if only for an hour or two, to reflect
On his life and ask him if he would
Intercede for us in our struggle here on earth. I suspect
He's in a better place now, for death is not the end.
We'll miss you, Dave. *Requiescat in pace*, my friend.

Dr. David Mack, 1936 – 2016.

John C. Dailey

"It matters not how strait the gate,
How charged with punishments the scroll,
I am the master of my fate:
I am the captain of my soul."
—William Ernest Henley, *Echoes iv*

Morior Invictus*

Preparations for another year of fighting
Were in process when our adversary struck
Unexpectedly. There had been no enemy sightings,
No sound was heard, and as luck

Would have it, there wasn't much damage.
I was embarrassed to be caught off guard.
Their attack last year was a rampage,
A devastating blow in our own backyard.

But we will prevail in the end.
We will not be overrun anymore.
I will gather my troops and send
A force that will decimate this foe.

How many years have we been fighting
These black-bearded killers of Christians and Jews?
Heartless butchers who slaughter and smite
In the name of Allah, who men of faith eschew.

I am not afraid of these fierce
Men, willing to die to bring chaos and grief.
I will not shirk from their hideous
Campaign against my beliefs.

I fight for a greater cause of freedom
For all men, even those of Byzantium.
I go forth 'neath the shield of the Paraclete,
And should I die, I die without defeat.

*Latin for " Death before Defeat."

John C. Dailey

Bill Lorenzen

I remember Bill Lorenzen.
Yes, I remember when
We first met in my office in Illinois,
In Jacksonville, when he was just a boy

About 40 years of age or so,
Tall and tanned, a friendly Joe.
He said he couldn't hear real well
And sometimes he had a dizzy spell.

I checked him out and did some tests,
Prescribed some pills to help him rest.
And finally found the answer if you please:
Bill suffered from Meniere's disease.

And though I was his doctor for awhile,
Our friendship took on a different style.
We shared our great love of the wilderness:
Canoeing and fishing and the rest.

When he moved north to River Falls
We still kept in touch with letters and calls.
His calmness and kindness live on in my mind:
My friend Bill was one of a kind.

So when we have gone to the other side
Where angels dwell and God presides,
Will we be remembered by those left behind?
Will they miss us? Will they even mind?

When I think that Bill is no longer here
I want to cry out, for I fear
My life will ne'er be complete.
I know that I will never meet

Another man like him. Oh Bill,
I'll miss you so. Tom, Chuck, and I will
Never share with you our tent
Or sit with you at dusk, all spent

From paddling hard against the wind and waves.
Sitting 'round the campfire, the night sounds stay
Within our hearts and minds, the voyageur's refrain.
I hope in another time and place, we'll be together once again.

My Friend Bill Lorenzen

My heart grows sad as I recall
My friend, Bill, who stood so tall.
I remember now when first I saw
Him. "Hello there," I heard him call.

His countenance all bright and clear,
His bearded face like a mirror,
Reflecting his great love of life.
Then something changed, some kind of strife.

It must have been some terrible pain,
A malevolent spirit that drove him insane.
What alien from hell invades our will
To make us not to want to live? Oh Bill,

A sadness fills my heart and mind
When I think of you who were so kind.
Oh Lord, can you bring him back sometime?
Let me see his face again before I too decline.

Two poems for Bill, 1945 – 2009

John C. Dailey

The End of the Portage

When I started this journey, the portage
Was easy and my pack was light, then
Something changed. Now I can barely manage
To carry the weight as I near the trail's end.
Why has this happened and who is to blame?
My hair has turned white and I feel strange,
And I know I don't look the same.
My body and I have become estranged.
I'm so weak and wasted but I keep on trying,
Though each day the pain gets more severe.
The Lord gives my soul rest for He knows I am dying.
I pray that the end of the portage is near.

I've finally come to the end of the trail, and I can see
Mom and Dad and my brother Jim, waiting there for me.

In memory of my cousin,
Charles "Chuck" Mertensotto
12/01/41 to 8/24/19.
A victim of exposure to
Agent Orange in Vietnam.

"Come to me all you who labor and are
burdened, and I will give you rest."

–Matthew 11:28

Agent Orange (AO)
(Or how I died from exposure to Agent Orange)

As I grew old and grey,
I wondered when the day
Would come that would be
My final one on this troubled sea

Of life. I've lasted all these years
In spite of all the usual fears
Of some unexpected calamity
Like a heart attack or disability.

Then something inside me changed.
It's like a part of me was being rearranged.
I felt strange, if that's the right term.
I didn't say much at first, maybe some germ

Had infected me and it would take a while
To go away. I drank chamomile,
And tried to ignore it; took pills from my cupboard,
Ate berries and kale, but I still felt weird.

My bloody red urine was the first alert.
That didn't resolve and began to hurt
When my water passed. Something ain't
Right. Will anyone listen to my complaint?

My doctor was too busy, I'm sorry to say;
Not like it used to be. But his nurse saved the day.
My vitals were checked. "Could be your prostate gland.
Blood and urine tests will help us understand."

John C. Dailey

There was blood in the urine. The prostate specific
Factor was over three hundred. She called to facilitate
An appointment with a specialist for a methodic
Exam to determine the status of my prostatic

Gland. It was enlarged and had a hard nodule.
After a painful biopsy with a special tool,
The results soon provided the answer:
"Your prostate gland is full of cancer."

All because I was drenched by Agent Orange
On my tour in Vietnam. They tried to expunge
The cancer the AO spawned but nothing
Helped. As it grows each day, I am praying

For relief. I'm withering away as this horrible
Menace gains control. The pain I feel is terrible.
I cry out in anger 'til the morphine sends
Me to a world of dreams. Will it ever end?

*In memory of my cousin, Army Sgt. Charles H. Mertensotto,
who served in Vietnam from 1966 -1968, and died of
prostate cancer in 2019*

Resident Days

We've gathered here now to honor him,
Our mentor and friend, Dr. Jim Brandenburg.*
It is fitting and proper to do this for Jim
So relax for a while and reflect on my words.

Dr. Jim worked hard and was always on call
Until it was time for his Army stint.
Then Nancy would pack his favorite golf ball
And with clubs in tow, we're not sure where he went.

I can still recall that very first day
When orientation was set to begin.
Drs. Bennett and Scott had to have the first say,
Then Kwaterski and Olson both chimed in.

"Now listen you guys, if you want to be smart
In the knowledge of ears, throats and noses.
With our stapes and septums we stand far apart
From toenails and rectums and compression hoses."

"Hey, Lange and Taborsky have got an admission.
Something is stuck in a nose; go find out what's in it.
Then Manhart and Scott need to make a decision.
Time is money, they say, so don't waste a minute."

The true test for us all was the VA,
Where we learned firsthand how the system was run.
Dr. Jim was in charge or so he would say,
But the ward clerk, Lou, said how things would be done.

John C. Dailey

While at the VA we learned new techniques,
Thanks to support from the guys from Green Bay.
Our surgical skills improved week by week,
And our patients were glad for their BM each day.

Back at the clinic on Bradley Two
Jim struggled to get the call schedule set.
With Hagan and Satz usually sick with the flu,
That left Diddams since Lonsdale had gone to the Met.

Some might suspect 'twas all work and no play,
And actually that was probably true.
Once we signed on and agreed to stay,
We worked twelve-hour shifts and ate hospital stew.

Was it worth it? You bet, no question at all.
Just look at us now, I insist.
Where once was a lamb afraid he might fall
You now see an Otolaryngologist.

*Chairman of the Dept. of Otolaryngology,
University of Wisconsin, on the occasion of his
Retirement, June 2000.*

The Seanchai

The old man with the weathered face
And aquiline nose sat in the room in a place
Reserved for special guests like him, a Seanchai,
A storyteller of Ireland's days gone by.

He was a lithe figure, a bit over six feet tall.
A long black coat and a wide brimmed hat was all
He wore against the elements as he walked alone
From place to place, his destination often unknown.

People came from all around
To hear his tales, listening to the sound
His words recalled, of St. Patrick, and the Navigator,
Of ancient New Grange, and the Norse invader.

After staying a few days in one locale
He moved on to another place, his rationale
Usually because of his underlying need
To pass on his stories before he might recede.

One day he set forth from Athlone on a county road
Toward Galway town and his next abode.
On the cobblestones of Quay Street, moistened
By the misty mix of fog and rain, he hastened

Past the shoppers and the colorful array
Of umbrellas moving about on the overcast day.
Not finding a place to rest his weary bones upon,
He moved thru town, his youthful days long gone.

He moved on toward Ennis town in County Clare.
Still wet from all the rain, his shelter was an ancient cave where

John C. Dailey

He hoped he'd find a better place, a friendly hearth,
Another home to tell a tale or two in the safety of a garth

Like the one in County Offlay at Clonmacnoise,
Where the Shannon casts a turquoise
Tint on sunny days, a quiet place where began
The Monastery founded by St. Ciaran.

He traveled near most everywhere in Ireland,
Year after year, from County Kildare and Monaghan,
To Tipperary and Meath and Donegal and Down;
And from Skibbereen city to Dublin town.

But he is no more, the times have changed.
Sadness penetrates his heart and he feels estranged
From this modern world of instant discovery,
Of fast cars and jet planes, and an ignorance of history.

Sleep*

Ah, sleep. Now who am I to say
What he has said so well,
That sleep doth heal
The cares and woes of life's travail?

For it is true that raveled sleeves
Of care no more will be,
Nor memories of bad deeds done
When sleep has worked its magic over thee.

Could there be more about
The healing power of sleep
That even Shakespeare failed to tell,
Something that we can't repeat?

Oh, weep for me ye who judge this rhyme
And forgive my bold attempt to spend your time.

Based on Macbeth, Act 2, scene 2

John C. Dailey

Late Afternoon in the Garden of the Pensione

It's late afternoon in the garden of the Pensione
Hohl in Gardone Riviera. Father Barreiro
Has finished his talk on El Greco and is holding his own
With Michael Davies, the same scenario

Repeated day after day, Father with his Campari
And Michael with his favorite Trentino Cabernet.
David White and John Rao are exchanging stories
While sipping their vodka with a vermouth bouquet.

The garden was small but large enough for the group
Attending the vonHildebrand Institute to enjoy cocktails
Before the evening repast of homemade Italian soup
And pasta complimented by locally grown varietals.

Moving back to the garden after dinner was a time to unwind
And enjoy each other's company before retiring for the evening.
For some, another glass of wine. For others it was a time
Of friendship and happy memories, a time for dreaming.

As I Walked Along the Country Road

As I walked along a country road
I stopped awhile and stood
And listened to the sounds
That gathered all around
Me: the quiet sound the breeze
Made as it danced thru the trees;
The rustling sound of corn leaves moving to and fro
As the wind whistled down along each row.
And then it was still again.

Except for an occasional truck or car
That passed by, I was all alone. To the south, far
Off, I heard the whistle of a train
As it moved along. Then it began to rain,
A gentle mist at first became a steady
Shower. Soon I was soaking wet and already
Looking for a place out of the rain when I spotted
The old covered bridge ahead and stopped
There to rest and dry out.

I must have nodded off, for the rain had passed.
The afternoon sun was shining and I noticed I cast
A shadow when I crossed the bridge to the other end
And stepped onto the rain-soaked road. Then
I started back the other way, back from where I'd come.
The sunlight warmed the humid air. Some
Horses in my neighbor's field moved near
The fence as I walked by. It was so quiet I could hear
Their tails swooshing as they brushed the flies off each other.

John C. Dailey

Sitting on the Porch on a Rainy Day

While sitting on the porch listening to the rain drops
Falling, I discovered the special sound
They make. And when the downpour finally stops,
I like to listen to the water dripping from the trees on to the ground.

The wetness in the warm air soon saturates my shirt.
Grey clouds fill the sky as more rain is on the way.
Before the rain I'd been planting flowers, and dirt
Was caked on my hands. I turned and started to say

Something to my wife when I heard a clap
Of thunder that followed a bright lightening flash.
The rain returned and our cat jumped into my lap.
I held her close but she jumped away and made a dash

For the open door into the house.
Cats are funny sometimes, fearful of sounds,
But run for your life if you're a mouse.
The shower passed and water was again dripping on to the ground.

My Back Yard

My back yard is a special place
With lots of trees and grass and space
To walk around and watch the birds,
And flowers, and sky. Sometimes words
Just aren't enough to say exactly how I
Feel inside. I look around and ask why?
Why am I so blest to be here
In this special peaceful place? There
Are not many places I would rather be.
For here I lose all sense of time, and see
Life from a different point of view.
Here I can briefly pause and renew
Myself and watch the humming birds flying
Back and forth at breakneck speed, charging
And darting from sugar-filled feeders to the tall pine tree
I planted long ago. At night I hear the symphony
Of insects singing. The lightning bugs flicker
As they meander back and forth, some quicker
Than the rest. Now I can hear the frogs join in
The chorus of the night sounds, and once again
I'm filled with wonder. I care very much for this space
For my back yard is a special place.

John C. Dailey

Spring

Oh, spring, you bring me joy.
You ease the heavy weight
Of winter's snow and cold.
You give me hope that new life
Will once again prevail.

January, 2022, by JCD

Vacation

Vacation time, what does it mean?
For most folks it's time to get away from
Home to go someplace where one can be seen
Cavorting about and having fun in the sun
On the beach. That makes sense as long as there
Is such a place. Actually, there are lot of choices
To pick from but don't make the mistake we
Made going to Myrtle Beach unless you like a lot of noises
From jet planes and helicopters and cars
And too many near-naked people.

A Summer Day

Oh how I love a summer day,
The breeze passing through the leaves,

The branches wave as if to say
"Don't you wish you could sway?"

And though I love a summer day,
I know that fall will soon be on the way.

John C. Dailey

Low Tide at Pawleys Island

The edge of the ocean seems far away
From where I sit by the sea oats
Covering the sand berm, constantly swaying
Back and forth in the breeze, afloat
In a sea of invisible power and might.

I can't see the wind but I can hear
And feel it as it rushes past me.
The waves roll in unceasingly like a fusilier
Battling a foe to victory,
As sunlight warms the white sandy beach.

Myrtle Beach

THE MYRTLE BEACH BEACH,
TOO CROWDED, NOISY, NOT NICE.
STAY HOME AND SAVE DOUGH.

Summer at Myrtle Beach

John C. Dailey

Iberia*

Iberia, the land of Spain,
Where Franco and his generals reigned.
A place where contrasts never end,
A place controlled by Rome's Churchmen.

From Visigoth, Moor, Jew and Greek
The Spanish heritage did keep
The best that each could give, and more,
And spiced the whole with pundonor.

Thru Michener's eyes we see this land
That spawned conquistadors so grand.
We see Badajoz and Madrid,
The bulls, flamenco and El Cid.

For one like you who's been to Spain,
This book recalls fond thoughts again.

*A sonnet based on the book, Iberia
by James A. Michener.*

Kilimanjaro

l have been called the "Mountain
Of Greatness," and other names too.
lt does not matter for it is certain,
l am known as the one who
ls the greatest and tallest of my kind
ln Africa and the world. l stand alone above all
Others. On a clear day l can see and find
The endless plains of Serengeti, and hear the call
Of elephants and lions, though they are far away.
l am a symbol of the majesty and flavor
Of Tanzania, where l live: yesterday
And today; tomorrow and forever.
lf what l have said proves to be untrue,
There is no sun or moon or sky of blue.

John C. Dailey

> "So dat's de reason I drink tonight
>   To de man of de Grand Nor' Wes',
> For hees heart was young, an hees heart was light
>   So long as he's leevin' dere—
> I'm proud of de sam' blood in my vein
>   I'm a son of de Nort' Win wance again—
> So we'll fill her up till de bottle's drain
>   An' drink to de Voyageur."
>
> —William Henry Drummond,
> from *The Voyageur and Other Poems*

John C. Dailey

Isle of Pines*

Nestled near the western end of Knife Lake,
On the Canadian border with Minnesota,
Is the Isle of Pines. "Knife Lake" Dorothy would make
Her home there from nineteen thirty until the
End of nineteen eighty-six, nearly fifty-six
Years. She lived alone most of that time,
Adopting a lifestyle that suited her, a mix
Of wilderness adventure and a new paradigm
Of social interaction. She was a beacon
Of light for all who stopped by
Her place by sled or canoe. For those seeking
Safe harbor, Dorothy's was a refuge,
If only brief, from life's deluge.

I can still see her in my mind,
Standing next to her wood-framed tent,
Her summer home. To find
Proper words to describe her slightly bent
Stature, her quiet demeanor, her subtle appeal,
Requires more than a simple comment
About her physical appearance. A grey-haired real-
Life lady who loved life, a peaceful
Woman whose kindness to all she met
Was long remembered after they left her beautiful
Island. They drank her root beer and went
On their way or maybe stayed awhile to sit
And talk. I'll remember and I won't forget.

*Known affectionately as "Knife Lake Dorothy,"
Dorothy Molter's Isle of Pines cabin was
located in the roadless wilderness area of the
BWCA, accessible only by snowmobile,
cross-country skis, snowshoes or canoe.*

Wilderness Day

I heard the water softly lapping
Up against the rocky shore and sensed
The gentle breeze upon my face as I lay napping
'Neath the fading sunlight, and all was quiet.

The sky above, so pure and blue,
With scattered cotton puff-like clouds.
The only sound, the wind blowing thru
The branches of the white pines 'round my tent.

How can I describe the feeling of that day?
The sense of serenity that all is well.
And if it were possible, I would rather stay
Here in the wilderness forever.

John C. Dailey

Wilderness Symphony

He first heard it in the canoe country up north.
He listened to the music, my old
Friend, Sig Olson, as he set forth
On his many trips into the woods. He told
Us he could hear a symphony of sounds:
The wind rustling the branches of the pines
And water rushing along as it pounds
Against the shore in a storm. The sign
That all is well when the haunting trill
Of the loons cavorting in the lake
Remind us that we are home again and feel the thrill
Of being once more in our wilderness escape,
The singing wilderness.

How does one describe the symphony,
The music of the wilderness,
Wherever it may be? It's not a cacophony
Of sound. It's more like a peaceful stillness.
Music that envelopes one and sooths
Life's burdens, cares and woes.
It is the absence of noise, whose
Presence ruins the equanimity that flows
From the tranquility of the quiet sound
Of silence. Most of the world has never heard
This symphony of which we speak nor found
The peacefulness they seek nor heard the words,
Of the singing wilderness.

John C. Dailey

A Quetico Day

The surface of Conmee Lake was like a mirror,
Reflecting the outline of our canoe.
The fading light reminding that sundown was near.
The haunting, mournful loon-song added to
The sense that peace and solitude were here.

Quietly, slowly we dipped our blades
Into the water and began to glide across
The lake. The canvas-covered hull was made
To slide easily on the smooth and glossy
Surface. All is still as daylight fades.

We landed the canoe by the rocky outcrop
Where we had earlier set up camp.
The air was cooler now so we stopped
To build up our fire. We were damp
From paddling and an unexpected shower of raindrops.

At first light we loaded the canoe with our packs,
The cargo evenly spaced 'tween bow and stern.
Paddling near shore, the wind at our backs,
We moved quickly at first then started to turn
Toward a distant point, always staying on track.

As paddlers we work as one
To propel the craft forward across the lake.
Both pulling back water, we began to hum
A voyageur's song, "A la claire fontaine..., *
And bathe in the warmth of the morning sun.

John C. Dailey

Our Seliga was made for this kind of trip,
Crafted with care of canvas and wood.
A solid vessel designed to slip
With ease in bad weather and good,
Through rough seas and calm, a seaworthy ship.

We soon reached the portage back in the bay.
While our canoe floated next to the land
The packs were unloaded and placed safely away
On the shore. Picking up our gear, the canoe tied to a stand
Of alder brush, we started down the trail on our way.

We hustled back for the canoe
And the rest of the gear. I flipped
It on to my shoulders. It wasn't too
Heavy, about eighty pounds. I slipped
On some rocks but carried it all the way through.

And so we continued for the rest of the day,
From portage to portage and from lake
To lake, stopping to rest now and then and to say
A prayer that no one would take
The campsite on Keefer where we planned to stay.

"At the clear running fountain..."

John C. Dailey

135

Tea on the Portage

The Ojibway woman was sad.
Tears dripped from her eyes and moistened her face.
Her baby was still nursing and now she had
To leave her village, her friends and family. "More space,"
Her husband said. "We need to go to a new
Place where we have our own *Weegiwahm*, our own home,
Where our son can build his birch bark canoe
And grow into manhood and be free to roam
All the lakes and forests of our people."

The woman stood by the canoe as her husband and son
Loaded their few belongings. She sat in the middle holding
The baby while her husband and son paddled. Everyone
In their village on Basswood watched as the canoe folded
Into the distant shoreline. A light breeze from the south
Helped to push them further along to the first portage,
To the lake where they planned to stay overnight. Smallmouth
Bass were spawning nearby, *noosa-owesi*, in the language
Of the Ojibway people.

They unloaded the canoe and started carrying their packs
Over the portage. Stopping to rest for a while
In a small clearing, father built a fire and then went back
For the canoe. Mother nursed the baby while their son piled
Up firewood. Hot tea warmed them and wild rice cakes
Satisfied their hunger. This first portage to the lake was long and uphill.
It was slow going with the baby, and even though her heart ached,
She did not complain. The second portage was easier. It was very still
As they paddled across the lake to their campsite on the point.

They were up at daybreak the next day but a heavy mist shrouded
The shoreline. They packed their gear and ate smoked venison
And tea. Soon the mist faded and they departed. Clouds
Filled the sky and it started to rain as they hastened
To the first portage where they stood under their canoe
Until the rain passed. They paddled for two days,
Always in the direction of the sunrise, until they came to
Kahshahpiwi, and as the light faded away
After sunset, they set up their camp for the night.

They rested for three days, eating fresh-caught fish, smoked bear
Meat and wild rice stew. Father was unsure which trail
To take but decided to go north through three lakes where
The fast water spilled out of Kawnipi, sailing
Through the Forks toward Snake Falls and the lake of many sturgeons.
They portaged around the rapids and rested by a large round
Lichen-covered rock, then on to a campsite where there was a profusion
Of blueberry bushes and firewood. The next day they paddled down
Kawnipi to the village in Kawa Bay.

This journey takes place in the late eighteen hundreds
In the area that we know today as the Quetico Provencial Park

John C. Dailey

The Colonoscopy

My pants are pulled down to my toes,
My arse exposed for all to see;
How then do you propose
To use that black snake hanging there?

Am I to hold it like a rope
To keep from falling to the floor?
If that's the case I pray and hope
It's strong enough to hold my weight.

You wouldn't try to force that
Thing into my body would you now?
It's much too big to swallow; where's my hat?
I want to go away.

Suddenly I'm so very sleepy.
What is it you have done to me?
This thing is getting rather creepy;
Where's my mommy when I need her?

"Would you like a drink?"
I heard a lady say.
I answered, "Yes" then stopped to think:
Have I been asleep or what?

Slowly I sat up and looked around,
Still groggy from my nap.
Then I heard a familiar sound.
"How are you, is everything ok?"

Old Shoes

I don't remember where I got them.
Maybe from a store back home.
But I wear them every day. They're
Scuffed and bruised; I can't recall when

I didn't wear them. You know how it goes:
When you find a pair that fit well,
No matter how bad they look, if your feet
Feel good the pleasure in your face shows.

Old shoes are like old friends.
You want to take good care of them,
Nurture them, and hope they last forever,
Like a special friendship that never ends.

John C. Dailey

Miss Gracie

I have a cat,
Miss Gracie. Actually, that
Is not quite right.
I think she might
Think that she has me
Because you see,
She tells me and my Missus
Whenever she wishes
Us to open the back door
So she can explore

The screened-in porch
And observe the approach
Of all the bugs and birds.
Then without any words,
She walks back inside
To find a place to hide
So she can sleep.
My, how does she keep
Up such a tireless pace?
Is it time to go to the place

Where we keep the treats?
The answer is yes! Nothing beats
A tasty snack
As she plans an attack
On a naïve mouse.
While she scouts the whole house,
She favors a spot
By the kitchen stove, not
That any place wouldn't do,
As long as she can pursue

A delicious meal. In a heartbeat is seems
She catches her mouse; then she rests and dreams.
Once she has her prey
She likes to play
With her new-found friend,
Soon to be her next meal in the end.
She likes to stretch out and sleep on her back
Before she plans her next attack.
And as she prepares for another quest,
The thing she likes best

Is to sit on mom's lap in the overstuffed chair,
Dreaming cat dreams without a care.
"Gosh, life's such a rat-race.
How can I keep up this torrid pace?"
At the end of the day,
When it's time to say
Good night, Gracie is there,
Sitting on the end of the bed, where
She snuggles up against mom's feet
While she does her bath. Oh my, she's so sweet.

Miss Gracie is a fluffy brown Siberian

John C. Dailey

The Dancing Horses

Round and round and round and round,
The carousel turned around like a giant bagel,
A spinning top moving to the sound
Of the calliope, sitting in the middle of a stable

Filled with galloping horses that moved
Up and down and round and round.
The music of the carousel filled the air,
Calling me back to a simpler time, the sound

Stirring up memories of long ago. Not a care
In the world, a time without time. I found
Myself reminiscing about my folks, and the county
Fair, and selling soda in the grandstand.

Sometimes life seems to be a merry-go-round
That never stops and we never get off.

John C. Dailey

The Bearded Lady

The bearded lady swirled
And swayed gently in the warm
Summer breeze. As she continued to twirl,
The wind started gusting and a storm

Began to form. She stood strong
As the sky darkened and the rain
Started to fall, dripping down from the long
Soft petals of her gown. She didn't complain,

For the shower seemed to enhance
Her natural beauty. As the rain gradually faded,
Sunlight filtered through the clouds and she danced
Again, celebrating the life for which she has waited.

As the last drops of rain filled the moisture-laden air
A rainbow formed. A quiet calmness
Reigned again in the garden. I couldn't help but stare
At my beautiful amarillo-colored bearded iris.

66

"A thing of beauty is a joy forever"

—John Keats, Endymion (1818) bk. 1

99

Water Lilies

The boat rested easily,
Rocking back and forth as gentle
Puffs of air swirled around, the breeze
Just enough to push it out of the channel
And into a multitude of water lilies
That covered nearly all the surface
Of the small shallow pond. To get free,
I pushed forward, trying to disperse
The tangled vines and great green pads
That floated on the water; I brushed aside their
Pink and yellow flowers, beautiful nomads
In the bright sunlight; I struggled, sadly aware
Of the havoc I had caused to escape. Finally free,
In open water, I rowed toward the small village of Giverny
That was ahead of me. On the shore I could see
A man painting. I asked his name but he wouldn't say.
I watched him for a while as he painted,
Quickly filling his canvas with blue and green pastels,
The composition emerging as the colors blended
Together, taking shape, swirling around like a carousel.

Many years have passed since that day in Normandy.
I can still see the bearded old man by the pond on one knee,
Painting the flowers floating on the water, the subtle harmony
So serene. I wonder whatever became of him?

Wind and Rain

Brother Wind and Sister Rain stayed the same
Year after year, doing what they were supposed to do.
They nurtured everyone and people came
From all around to be healed and renewed.
From a gentle breeze to a blustery puff,
Wind remained constant and steadfast,
Teaching and showing Rain all the stuff
She needed to know until at last
Rain was able to shower the people
With truth and love and all admired her.
Wind and Rain, working together, were usually able
To solve most of the people's problems; they were
A team. Then something happened. Her showers stopped
And became sprinkles for a while. Rain had changed.
Without telling Wind, she decided to move on and adopt
A new image. Then Sister Rain was gone; it was so strange.
Wind was devastated and lost without her.
He first felt confusion then anger then sadness and sorrow.
Wind kept blowing but without the healing water
Of Rain he'll never again climb Kilimanjaro.

John C. Dailey

Global Warming

GLOBAL WARMING—WHAT
A HOAX AND A JOKE—SCIENCE
NO—POLITICS YES

Spring in Minnesota

The Girl with the Pink Tattoo

The girl with the pink tattoo
On the back of her neck
Stood next to me on the crowded bus. Some blue
Was mixed with the pink, and a speck
Of yellow also highlighted the Skin
Artist's work, a beautiful bird. Then I saw what
Resembled a big brown spider on her chin
And a lacy web like a one-legged culotte
Wrapped itself around her left arm and elbow.
Gracing her right shoulder was a monkey,
His tail encircling her right arm, a Maracaibo
Capuchin. Her ill-fitting flimsy
Light green tank top seemed to conflict
With her dermal gallery ensemble.
But what does the artwork mean? Does it depict
A story or a message? Might it be permissible
To suggest there's a struggle for survival
Of the spider against the predatory
Bird and monkey? The spider's primeval
Instinct is to seek out the web, its sanctuary.
On the other hand, there may be no
Hidden meaning at all. Maybe she just likes monkeys
And birds, and arachnids that go
Crawling about spinning webs. If it were me,
I'd display that bird where I could see it every day.

While I grappled with these images to construe
Their meaning, the bus stopped;
She left and walked away,
The girl with the pink tattoo.

John C. Dailey

149

Part Four
Prayer, Faith, and Sin

St. John Fisher Was
Martyred, Tower Hill, London
Fifteen Thirty-Five

Part Four Contents

John C. Dailey

Introduction: Prayer, Faith, and Sin

This last collection showcases some thoughtful poems, my favorite being "The Portage Trail," which is the title of this book. A number of poems are meant to have a spiritual nature or quality. The last two are a commentary on the horrible practice of abortion. They are meant to be disturbing, even harsh, and I make no apology for them.

> "Hear my call for help,
>   my king and my God!
>   To you I pray, O Lord."
>
> —Psalm 5:3

> "Lord, do not trouble yourself for I am not
>   worthy to have you come under my roof.
>   Therefore, I did not consider myself worthy
>   to come to you; but say the word and my
>   servant will be healed."
>
> "I tell you, not even in Israel have I found
>   such faith."
>
> —Luke 7: 6-7; 9

> "...et veritas liberabit vos..."
>
> —John 8:32

John C. Dailey

The Soul

Where am I, as I looked around?
It was dark and warm and wet.
The last thing I recall was the sound
Of HIS glorious voice that sent

Peace and love to all; and then
In the next instant I'm here. Of course,
I should have known HE would send
Me sometime to be the source

Of life for His new creation, a man-child.
I am a human soul, an exact reflection
Of HIM. I was infused into the undefiled
Uniting of two cells at the moment of conception,

And life began. While man's body will die, even so,
I am life and will never death know.

The Battle for the Soul

The battle for the soul begins
When that first breath of air descends
Into the airless pulmonary space
And earthly life we doth embrace.

The evil one now sets his course
Lurking around, trying to force
The soul into a sinful state
Where love is gone, replaced by hate.

Ever since that first transgression
When pride took possession
Of Eve's soul, temptations wait for everyone,
To separate us from God's only Son.

As a child I knew not the ways of the world
Nor the sorrows and sadness of sin unfurled.
But I am older now and have encountered sin
And know it's a battle I must always win.

John C. Dailey

Garden Music

Napping by my backyard koi pond
On a glorious sunny afternoon,
Gentle puffs of wind were swirling 'round.
I was awakened by a strange musical tune.

No one was around or nearby
But I was sure I heard singing,
A beautiful acappella chorus of high
And low pitched voices bringing

Forth the most enchanting sound.
Where was it coming from I wondered?
I lay there quietly and listened, spellbound,
Afraid to move. Had I blundered

Into some secret vocal group harmonizing,
Practicing their music for a show?
I listened with care, suddenly realizing
The scene had changed. I didn't know

Where I was. The koi pond was not there.
I was lying on a soft grey mat.
The scent of orange blossoms filled the air
And the singing faded away as I sat

Up. My mat was resting on a narrow holm,
And a gentle voice welcomed me home.

Gunnar was in a good mood. The beautiful weather and the lack of pain that day helped, but it was more than that. He had come to the realization that he didn't need to be anxious about the future. He recalled what he had learned in his high school theology class with Brother Frank Clapp. It was one of his favorite passages in the Old Testament, Ecclesiastes 3:1-2:

For everything there is a season, and a time
for every matter under heaven:
a time to be born, and a time to die;

—*The Story of Gunnar Hansen*

The Portage Trail

There is a secret portage trail
Known to but a few,
Nestled in a forest vale,
Glistening in the morning dew.

As I walked along that path, a gentle breeze
Enhanced the sound of quiet all around.
I spied a shaft of light beaming thru the trees
And looked to where it landed on the ground.

At first I couldn't see the place
Because of all the brush and rocks nearby.
Then I looked off to my left and traced
The light up to a ledge of rock on high.

Carefully, I moved thru all the brush and climbed up there,
And found an unexpected sight.
A single flower had taken root within that lair
Where the mor and soil could catch the light.

I wiped the sweat from off my face
And tried to catch my breath.
My first thought was that in my haste
I had disturbed that precious growing cleft.

But no, my movement had not upset the flower.
She stood tall and strong, catching the first rays of light
While drops of morning dew dripped like a shower
On to the soil beneath, both left and right.

John C. Dailey

I can't explain the scene that I beheld,
A sublime reflection of the mystery of the Three:
A single bloom atop a long green stem did dwell,
With three pink petals round one rose pouch, like the Trinity.

I gazed upon her for a minute more,
Enhanced by her regal stance.
How had I missed her when I'd passed this way before?
Had she always been there waiting for my glance?

That must have been the case.
For I'd traversed this trail so many times,
Usually rushing to some other place,
Not stopping much to look at all the signs.

Then I began to take my leave
And start back on the track.
I wondered, "Should I take the flower with me,
Or leave her here 'til I come back?"

That thought passed quickly from my mind
As I walked along the portage trail.
For I knew she could not survive the kind
Of trip ahead: without proper care she would surely fail.

I've gone back many times since that special day
To view my hidden beauty once again.
With petals smooth and soft she seems to stay
Forever young and fresh and without stain.

" "The Christian ideal has not been tried
and found wanting. It has been found
difficult and left untried."

—G.K. Chesterton:
What's Wrong With The World, 1910, pt, 1 **"**

" "It is harder for some people to believe that God
loves them than to believe that he exists."

—Basil Hume, English Cardinal
Guardian 18 June, 1999 **"**

Tomorrow

If tomorrow should never come to be
And you had just this day to live,
In looking back, what would you see?
Does the thought that your life will end this day
Ever enter your mind
As you fritter about, seldom stopping to pray?
How often have you done a good deed
For no reason at all,
Except for the fact there was someone in need?

Can you provide
A good account of your life?
Would you be forthright or try to hide
Your tragic flaws? No matter how hard you try
To conceal them, the facts of your life
Will always be there when you die.
Are you prepared to accept His request
To relinquish your life?
When that happens will you pass the test?

John C. Dailey

The Atheist

Do you know any atheists?
Do you think they exist?
I'm asking the question because I'm not sure
If anyone of that persuasion could endure

The truth. If you don't believe in
God and don't acknowledge sin
Or miracles or life after death,
Or any future when you breathe your last breath,

Then the atheist must lead a dismal, lonely
Life. There may be worldly wealth and fame but only
For a fleeting moment in time, and then nothingness.
But it doesn't have to be that way. Just listen once

To Him who created and loves you
And wants you to be with Him forever. Who
Waits patiently while you dither and dance
In utter confusion. Believe this: it did not happen by chance.

"Hello, My atheist friend, are you there?
I wanted to let you know that I am here.
You silly fool, just where did you think I would be?
I've been here waiting for all time, for you see,

It's like this: I AM."

Eternal

There is no beginning and no end, only now, because
There was no yesterday and there is no tomorrow, only today.
There is no time as we know it because the Creator always was
And always will be. It is correct to say

This is because the Cause of it all, the Creator, is an invisible,
Indescribable, incomprehensible, spiritual being
Who has always existed; an incontrovertible
And undeniable all-knowing Truth, unvarying

And impossible for a human mind to understand.
How can that be you ask, timelessness
In a world engulfed in time? We'd be a no-man's-land,
A void without time. This is the age-old enigma, to confess

Our ignorance of this mystery of life.
And more, the mystery of the afterlife.

John C. Dailey

The Golden Years

Was it only yesterday when I was strong and fit and young?
What has caused this change that I'm not me anymore?
Where I was strong, I'm now weak. If I try to run,
My breathing quickens, can't get enough air like before.

Light headedness begins and I must rest before I fall.
My heart beats in a strange way that medicine
Cannot allay. Oh, Lord I pray you will forestall
This pattern of demise. I pray this is not the time when

You are calling me. And yet I feel my time in this life
May be coming to an end. I will never be the same again.
It's hard to face the reality of change. Yet the knife
That cuts our ties to this world opens the path then

To enter a new and better place, one where I will never
Die. My soul will rest in the bosom of eternal life forever.

Our Lady

Falling, falling, slowly falling,
White-glazed drops of water falling
All around. Oh listen to Our Lady calling,
"Children Come To Me."

Her voice is so sublime and pure,
Her beauty unequaled far and near.
The meaning of her plea is clear:
"My Children Come To Me."

By throwing off our grown up ways
And taking up our childhood days
We once again can sing our praise
Of Love for Mother Mary.

John C. Dailey

The Golden Dome

Oh Lady on the Golden Dome,
Standing there for all to see.
Shining bright above your home
In all your glorious subtlety.

Queen of angels, Queen of peace,
Our Mother she'll forever remain.
With gentle arms she doth embrace
Her sons and daughters of Notre Dame.

The Legacy of Father Ted

How sad it is to see,
What's happened to our University.
Dedicated to the Mother of us all,
Who stands above us in her Golden stall.
How we ask, did this come about?
It happened because of one man's doubt
That God alone was not the route
To power and prestige in this secular
World. He placed his faith in another,
The angel, Lucifer, to light his way to fame,
And told the Pope, "We'll be the same;
We just don't want you telling us what to do.
Academic freedom is our goal. Rome, you
Aren't needed any more." His sad legacy
Lives on as Notre Dame's respectability
As a bastion of Catholic Culture is no more.

John C. Dailey

Flying

As you navigate your earthly flight,
Keep true the course with all your might.
For sin will take you far away
From Him who gave His life that day.

As your soul soars to unknown heights
With the goal of heaven in her sights,
Pray you'll live forever more
With Him on Elysium's sheltered shore.

Change

Oh change, I wish that you would go away
And let things always stay
The same. It is so difficult
To see the end result
When things never stay the same.

I want to lash out and blame
Someone or something; but who to name?
Who causes the discord when
Equanimity is uprooted and then
We have to start all over again?

John C. Dailey

The Dove

Friend of Jesus that you are,
Leaving your home and traveling far
To my home to share your love.

My thanks to you for bringing the Dove,
The product of His Knowledge and Love.
You surely must know Him well.

Like the deaf child who tripped and fell,
I stayed on the ground. I couldn't yell
For help because I had no speech.

My voice would tremble as I would reach
The threshold of sound, but only a screech
Came forth, and no one could understand.

Now my ears are clear. His hand
Had opened the tubes. The sound is so grand
As I hear His voice calling me.

The tears of joy that dripped like the sea
And tasted of salt, now seem to be
Like a fine vintage wine: full of warmth and love.

And dear friend as we bid goodbye,
Remember me and I
Will remember you.

A New Day

At first light, before the sun appears,
The eastern sky begins to glow. I stand in wonder
As the earth becomes bright and clear
And the world awakens from its nighttime slumber.

As the day begins and I embrace
The wonder of the dawn,
Sunlight begins to warm my face
As I marvel at the newborn morn.

Once again the cycle of the sun
And moon has been fulfilled.
A new day has begun,
In accordance with our Creator's will

John C. Dailey

A Song for Opus Dei
(The Spirit of the Work)

Let me begin this simple tale
By greeting you my God, my Lord.
For through your guidance will prevail
The goodness of our just reward.
How can I tell Thee how I feel?
The words are locked inside my skull.
The vivid images are real,
Mere thoughts that only might enthrall
The spiritual gift we all possess,
Our Soul. And so I'll try as best I might
To form the words and so address
The subject about which now I write.

Josemaria knew you well,
Your Spanish soldier fighting sin.
His love for you helped him to tell
The world to sanctify itself to win.
"Through you, Lord, the Work was begun,"
Monsignor Escriva would say.
You picked your native Spanish son
To start this thing called, "Opus Dei."
From Calle Ferraz in old Madrid
Where young men first the Father met,
The Work has spread and helped to rid
Confusion in a world by sin beset.

To you, Josemaria, is due,
For words sublime and pure and true,
A heartfelt thanks, our prayers, our new
Resolve: A life of alabaster hue.
For saints we all must strive to be
Though this may seem a goal too far.
Our Father taught us how to see
Sainthood is not some distant star.
Don Alvaro, Don Javier
Sons of the Father, prelates both
Leading the Work along The Way,
Widening The Furrow, affirming their oath.

John C. Dailey

CHIANTI
JOHN DAILEY

A Noble Drink

It was a pleasant day
In the Garden as I recall.
My family and I hoped to stay
There forever; but it wasn't to be. Adam's fall
Changed everything. We were told to leave
That earthly paradise, vines and all. Then the Voice
Spoke to me and said, "I will offer a reprieve
For you and yours but you have to make a choice
To freely accept a task I have in mind for you."

I thought, why would He want to bother?
We're just lowly grapes living on a vine. Do
We have any worth? He must have the answer.
So I said, "Yes, yes, we accept; we will serve thee."
Immediately we found our vines growing
On a sunny hillside near an ocean, the sea
Breeze gently bathing us and then flowing
Back from where it came. That's when
I heard the Voice again: "Because you have

Served me well, I will make you revered by all men.
The fruit of your vines will be worth more than just to salve
The hunger of the creatures of my creation. Take heed,
For the juice from your fruit will be the noble drink
For all mankind. It will perform a special deed
That will be the salvation for all men, the link
To eternal life with me in heaven." Those words were
The answer to the purpose of our mission begun long ago:
To bring forth the wine that Jesus consecrated at the Last Supper.

John C. Dailey

Torreciudad*
En el Paseo al Hermita

Sitting by the perfumed path
With scent of pine trees wafting aft,
I spied an angel gliding by
And thought how near am I

To You, Oh Lord, my guiding light.
And as I looked off to my right
I viewed the tower and esplanade
That are our Torreciudad.

I heard Your call on rushing wind
And felt Your sunlight's warmth begin
To calm my fear
And knew that You are near.

In this place of peace and prayer
Your mother rests upon her chair,
With alabaster all around,
Listening to the pleasing sound

Of tolling bells and rosary beads,
Extolling her to intercede
For them who love her so. For
Her love for You is evermore.

**Marian Shrine in Aragon*

Our Troubled World

The world is in pain,
So much suffering and unrest.
Will it ever be the same
As it was when we were blest
With peace, when there wasn't hate
And revenge and people killing
One another? Wouldn't it be great
If all of this would end, if we were willing
To take steps to stop it all? But how,
How would that be possible, given
Who we are: weak-willed men who scowl
At the very idea of compromise, driven
By our inherent selfishness? Ah, perhaps
That's too harsh, too critical. Good folks
Exist who want to prevent the collapse
Of our world, who have dreams and hopes
For a better life, who want to restore sanity
In an insane world. Our greatest weapon
To win this battle is prayer, a plea
To the Almighty, and faith that it will happen.
The second, some say, more practical way
To win the fight against our enemy,
Radical Islamic terrorism, is to simply say
"No more," and destroy it completely.

John C. Dailey

Tower Hill

The man, gaunt and grey, climbed the stairs
Of the scaffold slowly, his body weak
And wasted from a year in the Tower. Saying his prayers,
He read from John, 17:3-4, and took a moment to speak

To those gathered 'round to watch his execution.
On twenty-two June, 1535, Cardinal John Fisher,
Bishop of Rochester, a victim of persecution
By King Henry VIll, was beheaded. In spite of pressure

To take the Oath of Succession, John Fisher refused.
He informed Henry that his marriage to Catherine of Aragon
Was valid and thus was brought to trial and accused
Of treason for opposing Henry, who wanted a son

To succeed him. Henry then married Ann Boleyn, a royal
Courtesan known to Henry. Four wives later,
And no male successor, Henry died, a selfish, disloyal,
Despicable man. The Defender of the Faith became a traitor

To the Faith, started his own church and persecuted
The few Faithful left in England, including both
Thomas More, who also died on Tower Hill, executed
By beheading, and John Fisher. Neither would take the oath.

*Thomas More and John Fisher, martyrs for the Faith, were
Canonized Saints of the Church in nineteen thirty-five.*

The Great Heresy

It all began about six-hundred ten Anno Domini
And hasn't stopped, the on-going war
Against the heresy of Islam. Christian armies
Have come and gone and failed. More
Than a million men fought in the Crusades
In the 11th and 12th centuries and failed
To recover the Holy Land. The great parade
Of men and arms couldn't hold Jerusalem, and sailed
Home beaten. But before and after these
Epic ventures, a few battles were fought and won
And for a time there was victory for Christendom.

The sounds of battle raged through the night
As warriors of the Holy Cross carried the fight
Against the Moors of Emir Raman in seven thirty-two
At Tours. Led by Charles Martel, the Christian army slew
Their foe and stopped the advance of Islam.
"Fight on, fight on," Charles shouted 'ore the din
And dust of the Saracen advance. The Franks stood firm,
The Muslims fled and France was saved for Christendom.

While victory reigned in Tours that day,
Eight centuries more of war paved the way
For Don Juan of Austria and the Battle of Lepanto.
With a smaller force of men and ships, the Ottoman foe
Was soundly trounced off the coast of Greece and Don Juan,
The bastard son of Charles the Fifth, led the force that won
On that October day in fifteen seventy-one. Rome
And the west were saved for Christendom.

John C. Dailey

Though battle weary and beaten once again,
The Turks rearmed and hoped to win:
Another day, another place, another time.
The cry of "Allahu Akbar", their nauseating victory whine
Filled the dusty air as they marched
To the gates of Vienna, tired and parched.
Five score and twelve years since Lepanto, Jan Sobieski won,
Halting their advance, saving Europe for Christendom.

Sixteen centuries after Muhammad, we face a more intolerable
Foe, ISIS, who wars against all religions of the world,
Whether Buddhist, Hindu, Christian or Jew. This awful
Presence, using the Koran, has unfurled
A plan of radical jihad in the name of their demonic being, Allah.
This brand of Islam is nothing but a cult of hate
Against all unbelievers, the infidels. For Christians, the
Path to victory and peace is not to negotiate.
Our goal must be to decimate and obliterate and demand
Unequivocal surrender, not compromise.
We must be aware of the present danger, and
So what we see below will not be a surprise.

The swarthy-faced man stood
Outlined against the setting sun,
His automatic rifle ready, should
He need it. Darkness soon enveloped him, and some
Of his group set their guns aside,
Hoping to refresh themselves before engaging
The Iraqi infidels who were trying to hide
In their miserable little village. "With the battle raging
All around, these Christians continue to resist,
But not for long. This jihad will succeed!
The holy war for submission, for all to subsist
In the arms of Allah, in Sura nine, has been decreed."

In our battle against Islam do we have a choice?
For sixteen-hundred years, more or less,
Non-Muslims have shouted in a loud voice,
Their opposition. One can only guess
How many on both sides have died.
If Islam is a religion, it is not a religion of peaceful
Communion with other religions. We have tried.
But a true, non-violent Muslim, must be able
To put the Koran aside if he is to live in harmony
With his "infidel" neighbors. To borrow a line
From Hamlet*, "ay, there's the rub."* How can he be
Friends with non-Muslims, and worship at Allah's shrine?

*Shakespeare: Hamlet III, 1, 56

John C. Dailey

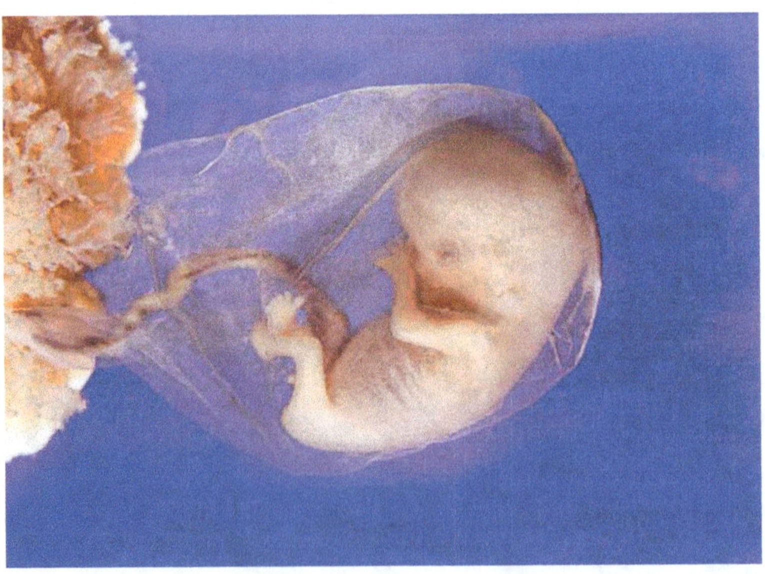

The Portage Trail and Other Journeys

The Clinic Visit

Her eyes revealed her fear,
Her sense of desperation.
What should she do? She could hear
Her parent's angry words. They had no appreciation
For how she felt: confused, alone and sad.

She hesitated before going in, then she pushed open
The door. The Clinic lady asked for her name
And the cash. Even though she was heartbroken,
She had made up her mind. Things will be the same
Afterward, she kept telling herself.

She suddenly felt chilled and she had to pee.
They told her where to go but to hurry;
She was next and the doctor had to be
At a luncheon meeting by noon. Don't worry
They said. You'll be fine.

The nurse helped her undress, then she lay
Down on the cart and they pushed her
Into a room where she was to stay
For a few minutes. Her vision was unclear,
Probably from the pill she'd been given.

Now it was her turn; the doctor sat at the end
Of the cart and lifted the sheet. She felt a sharp
Pain in her groin then she was numb; she began to bend
Her legs as he spread them apart. Just then, in her heart
She knew it was wrong but it was too late.

John C. Dailey

Her dead baby girl lay there in a dirty metal pan
Where she had been tossed
By the grey-haired, smiling man,
The doctor in the white lab coat. Her baby had lost
Her battle for life.

Her tiny body with her perfectly shaped
Fingers and toes, was splattered with the blood
Of her mother, from whose womb she was scraped
And crushed, then discarded ignominiously with a thud
By the smiling grey-haired man.

It was done. She lay there weeping. Weak
And confused, she asked if her baby was alright,
Forgetting that she wasn't in the delivery room. She tried to speak
Again but was told to be quiet. A bright light
Came on and they told her to get dressed and leave.

Business Lunch

The soothing voice of Sinatra blended
With the clinking of the dishes and silverware
And the soft hum of conversations that never ended.
She liked this place for the ambience and their
Sophisticated cuisine and wine list. Arrogantly shabby,
A good choice to enjoy lunch, a glass of wine
And discuss business. With all the stress, she was happy
To relax with her favorite Chardonnay. A sign
On the table noted today's special was romaine
With lite poppyseed dressing and sole almandine.

The food and wine were wonderful as usual,
But it was time to discuss the pending sale.
"The baby parts business is always brisk; the refusal
Of that last group to place an order failed
Because they just wanted kidneys and hearts.
The present client wants whatever is available,
And we only accept cash. We package the body parts
Fresh in Zip-Lock bags. We make them more salable
By packing two arms, two legs, one heart and one liver
Per bag. We're very proud of the product we deliver."

She couldn't resist another glass of the Chateau
Montelena. "Dickering over the price
For the various types of tissue you know
Will be trying so it's always nice
To soften the stress with a glass of wine.
This buyer also wants a full-term lad
And is willing to pay the price. That's fine.
For legs only, we have to leave a gonad
Attached so they know it's a boy.
It's a lot of work but it gives me great joy."

John C. Dailey

Dr. Gudrun Himmler paid the check and left a meager
Tip. She went outside to complete the sale:
The bags of parts for the cash. She was eager
To return to the Clinic as she needed a full-term male
To complete the order. There was someone
She examined yesterday, but she was too far along.
"Ah, no matter, we'll call her back and get the job done.
Her sono showed a beautiful boy, nice and strong."

Arrangements were made. "The young woman
With the full-term boy will return
Tomorrow and we'll dispose of her son."
Dr. Himmler was pleased, knowing she would earn
A real killing from the sale.
Just another day at the Clinic where mass murderers
Posing as doctors and nurses, assail
Their victims. Bereft of conscience, they are Satan's executioners.

Credits

Front cover, "Tea on the Portage," watercolor painting by John Peyton. Reproduced with permission, Hawk Ridge Art, Duluth, MN.

Back cover, "Lady Slipper Collage," by John Peyton. Reproduced with permission, Hawk Ridge Art, Duluth, Minnesota.

Bible quotations from the New American Bible, copyright 1970 by the Confraternity of Christian Doctrine.

Page 2 "Crossed Paddles" from public domain.

Page 12 "Irises," watercolor by John C. Dailey.

Page 19 "Picture of Robin," from public domain.

Page 24 "Miss Jane," photograph by John C. Dailey.

Page 31 "Jane," watercolor and crayon drawing by Jane Rottjakob, age six.

Page 55 "Coming Home for Christmas," Original painting by David Tutwiler. Reproduced with permission, David Tutwiler Fine Art: david@tutwilerfineart.com

Page 60 "Lady Slipper Collage," by John Peyton. Reproduced with permission, Hawk Ridge Art, Duluth, Minnesota.

Page 67 "Picture of Pat," reproduced by permission, Bill Wade Photography, Jacksonville, Illinois.

Page 71 "Red Rose," photograph by John C. Dailey.

Page 76 "Miss Grace," oil painting by Mary Sadaj.

Page 84 "Miss Gracie," watercolor by Mary Sadaj.

Page 93 "The Lady and the Knight," oil painting by Diane Schleyhahm.

Page 95 "Indian Head," oil painting on canoe paddle by John C. Dailey.

Page 114 "Rainy Day on Quay Street," photograph by John C. Dailey.

Page 116 "Pensione Hohl," photograph from the Public Domain.

Page 122 "Sea Oats" photograph by John C. Dailey.

Page 123 "Summer at Myrtle Beach," photograph by Matthewtrudeauphoto, WikiMedia Commons.

Page 127 "Portrait of Dorothy Molter," oil painting by John C. Dailey.

Page 130 "Silhouette of Pat at Dusk, Brent Lake, Quetico Park," photograph by John C. Dailey

Page 132 "Paddling in the Quetico," watercolor by John Peyton. Reproduced with permission, Hawk Ridge Art, Duluth, Minnesota.

Page 134 "The author in his Seliga canoe, Moose Lake, BWCA, 1958," photographer unknown.

Page 135 "Tea on the Portage," watercolor painting by John Peyton. Reproduced with permission, Hawk Ridge Art, Duluth, MN.

Page 139 "My Shoes," charcoal drawing my John C. Dailey.

Page 142 "Miss Gracie," photograph by John C. Dailey.

Page 143 "Carousel Horse," photo by James Veenstra. Reproduced with permission, JVee Graphics, Jacksonville, Illinois.

Page 145 "Bearded Iris," photograph by John C. Dailey.

Page 146 "Water Lillies," oil painting by Monet from the Public Domain.

Page 148 "Snowy Road," photograph by John C. Dailey.

Page 150 "Carousel Horse Head," photo by James Veenstra, Reproduced with permission, JVee Graphics, Jacksonville, Illinois.

Page 152 "St. John Fisher," oil painting by the Carmelite Nuns of Jesus, Mary and Joseph, Valparaiso, Nebraska. Reproduced with permission.

Page 160 "Solo Portage," pen and ink drawing by John Peyton. Reproduced with permission, Hawk Ridge Art, Duluth, Minnesota.

Page 163 "Lady Slipper," photograph from the public domain.

Page 170 "The Golden Dome," photograph reproduced with permission, Public Affairs Office, University of Notre Dame, Notre Dame, Indiana.

Page 172 "F-15 Eagle," picture from public domain.

Page 178 "Wine Bottle," oil painting by John C. Dailey.

Page 185 "Eight-Week Fetus," photograph from Priests for Life website, Fr. Frank Pavone, reproduced with permission.

Page 192 "John C. Dailey," photograph by Ken Casey.

John C. Dailey

The Miracle

l stared in abject horror
As he fell to the floor of the dais
Amid popping sounds and shouts.

My heart stopped for a moment
And l cried out, "Oh, NO,
Our President has been shot."

Oh, God, l prayed it isn't so . . .
And then, lifted up by angels
With blood on his face and fist

Raised high in triumph over death,
Saved by God's good grace,
President Trump marched to victory.

July 13, 2024

John C. Dailey is a graduate of the University of Notre Dame and the University of Illinois College of Medicine. After serving two years in the Navy, he completed a Residency in Otolaryngology at the University of Wisconsin. He lives in Jacksonville, Illinois. Dr. Dailey retired from the practice of medicine in 2022. He and his wife live in Jacksonville, Illinois.

www.ingramcontent.com/pod-product-compliance
Lightning Source LLC
Chambersburg PA
CBHW051828150726
47998CB00001B/335